ROGER STEVENSON
FEBRUARY, 1995

The United States of Incompetence

Books by Art Carey

IN DEFENSE OF MARRIAGE
THE UNITED STATES OF INCOMPETENCE

The United States of Incompetence

Art Carey

HOUGHTON MIFFLIN COMPANY / BOSTON / 1991

For information about permission to reproduce selections from
this book, write to Permissions, Houghton Mifflin Company,
2 Park Street, Boston, Massachusetts 02108.

Library of Congress Cataloging-in-Publication Data
Carey, Art.
The United States of Incompetence / Art Carey.
    p.   cm.
Includes bibliographical references.
ISBN 0-395-57039-5
1. United States — Social conditions — 1980–   2. United
States — Moral conditions.   3. United States — Economic con-
ditions — 1981–   4. Performance.   I. Title.
HN59.2.C37   1991   91-11597
306'.0973 — dc20   CIP

Printed in the United States of America

Book design by Lisa Diercks

BP 10 9 8 7 6 5 4 3 2 1

FOR G.P.

Contents

Introduction

I AM PROUD of the United States and glad to be an American, but in recent years I've become worried about this nation and pessimistic about its future. Much of my anxiety stems from the nearly unbelievable tales of incompetence that confront me every time I pick up the newspaper. But my concern is fueled even more by everyday encounters with ordinary people — fellow Americans who don't do what they're supposed to do or, even worse, *won't* do what they're supposed to do.

One or two instances a month I could handle. But the incompetence I run into almost every day is so dismaying — and often so enraging — that there are times when I feel like climbing to the top of a tall building and, like Howard Beale, the demented anchorman in *Network*, shouting, "I'm mad as hell and I'm not going to take it anymore."

I am not alone, of course. No doubt you picked up this book because you too are disgusted by incompetence and still fuming about the awful experiences you've had with incompetent people and inferior products. Usually, we just shake our heads or sigh in disbelief, convinced there is nothing we can do. It's the price of progress, the down side of democracy, and after all, as everybody knows, you can't fight City Hall.

Meanwhile, the nation continues to slide.

I can't watch that happen and keep my peace. I am not by nature a crusader. I am not a flag waver, and I have no appetite for causes. But I do care about this nation — a precious historical accident many of us fail to appreciate — and I do care about America's future and the kind of world I'll leave behind for my children. Hence, this polemic, this proud jeremiad.

But some may wonder how anyone can gripe about American incompetence after the astounding success of Operation Desert Storm. Our soldiers were well trained and impressively professional. Most of the high-tech weaponry the Pentagon has spent billions on not only worked but, in some cases, worked amazingly well. Moreover, the brass plotted the war so ably that, in one fell swoop, they banished the specter of Vietnam, restored pride in America's armed services, and fostered new respect for U.S. military muscle around the world. But just because we beat up a tinhorn dictator like Saddam Hussein doesn't mean that suddenly everything in America is dandy. Our Persian Gulf victory made most of us deliriously patriotic precisely because such spectacular demonstrations of U.S. competence have lately been so rare.

Look at it this way: We are like a high school whose physical plant is falling apart because it's been neglected for years. Our school is always broke and must borrow to pay its bills. Our principal is nice but more interested in district affairs than in crises in his own building. Our vice principal is pretty but a ridiculous dunderhead. Our teachers are constantly bickering and more concerned about their own tenure and perks than about serving us. We students are ignorant, fractious, destructive, and violent, riven by race, class, and money into hostile tribes. We cheat, we steal, we take drugs, and more and more often we are killing each other. Our morale is low and sinking lower.

Then, after a long drought, our football team manages to crush a cocky but outgunned opponent. Hail the conquering heroes! We are awash in school spirit, so wildly jubilant we forget all our divisions and problems. In time, however, the euphoria fades, and the problems, we find, are still there — as formidable and intractable as ever.

This book grew out of an article I wrote for the *Philadelphia Inquirer Magazine*. That article, in turn, grew out of a conversation over lunch with some of my colleagues. During that cathartic meal, someone recounted an infuriating episode caused by incompetence, and soon we were all swapping yarns about our own run-ins with incompetent people and crummy products. Everybody had stories to tell, and everybody told them with such fervor that we soon realized we had stumbled onto something, that we had the makings of a story that might strike a universal chord.

As I began talking to people — ordinary folks as well as teachers, professors, historians, sociologists, psychologists, economists, essayists, commentators, and authors — it became abundantly clear that our lunchtime hunch was correct, that indeed there is a great deal of discontent with what America has become and where America is heading. Later, when my essay about incompetence was published, it provoked the largest reader response in the magazine's history — more than two hundred letters, innumerable telephone calls, and scores of requests for reprints.

This book is a continuation of that essay. It is also an account of my exploration of the state of the nation in the last decade of the so-called American century. It is laced with many of my own experiences, opinions, and musings about the disappointments and failings of contemporary society. It also contains plenty of eloquent and substantiating testimony from experts, informed observers, and just plain regular people who are equally worried about the condition of the United States today and the spiritual sickness that has clouded our vision and hindered our efforts to sustain the tradition of excellence established by our forebears.

I do not have any ideological ax to grind (for the record, I'm a registered Democrat, but some of my best friends are Republicans). Incompetence is a disease of conservatives and liberals, the rich and poor, the upper class and the underclass, management and labor, Ivy League grads and high school dropouts, white and black, old-stock Americans and just-arrived immigrants. Its manifestations are as diverse as the United States itself; it is, indeed, an all-American ailment.

I hope that everyone who reads this book becomes angry, too — angry enough to do something about it. Of course, I'm prepared for the fact that, in the end, some of the anger will be directed at me, the messenger bringing the bad news. Some liberals will think I'm a fascist; some blacks will think I'm a racist; some conservatives will think I'm a brash and disrespectful iconoclast, reveling in the negative, failing to give America credit for its many virtues and accomplishments.

So be it. I am not a pollster or a social scientist. I am not an intellectual. I am a reasonably alert, conscientious citizen with some measure of common sense, a low tolerance for sham and hypocrisy, the ability to report what I see, the foolhardiness to say what I think, and the means to publish my views — not "the truth," but my views, for I know the truth is much larger and more subtle than anything I can discern.

Nevertheless, I make no apologies, for I'm convinced that my main thesis is indisputable — namely, that incompetence is rife in the United States today and an abiding, corrosive aggravation in the lives of most Americans. What's most terrifying is that incompetence is like a plague; if left unchecked, it will spread from the individual to the organization, infecting the next generation, growing more virulent at every stage, until our nation is unable to function. Each encounter with incompetence undermines our expectations, numbing us to the possibility of excellence, wearing down our resistance to poor performance, making us more apprehensive about having to depend on others.

That's the bad news.

The good news is that a heartening number of us realize that the epidemic of incompetence afflicting the United States must be recognized and dealt with now, before it's too late. I hope that this book, by sounding an alarm, helps.

The United States of Incompetence

1 "Things Fall Apart"

I T IS just a bridge, a simple two-lane bridge.

Until recently, it carried a busy road — Bowman Avenue — over the railroad tracks that give the Main Line, the swank, leafy suburbs west of Philadelphia, its name.

There is nothing special about this bridge, except that my neighbors and I depend on it to travel from one side of the community to the other. There is nothing special about this bridge, except that the Pennsylvania Department of Transportation allowed it to deteriorate so badly that in the fall of 1988 inspectors declared it unsafe and suddenly closed it. There is nothing special about this bridge, except that because of bureaucratic wrangling it won't be replaced, at the earliest, before the fall of 1991, three years since it was shut. As a commissioner in the township where the bridge is located griped, "The bridge over the River Kwai was built in less time."

There is nothing special about this bridge, except that every time I want to use it, and can't, my blood starts to boil, especially since, in all that time, during many inconvenient months, no matter what the hour or day, I've never seen a single person working on it.

What the hell is going on here?

Why is it that in one of the richest townships in one of the richest counties in one of the richest nations in the world — a country that once gloried in its engineering derring-do — we can't rebuild a simple two-lane bridge in under three years?

Where is Teddy Roosevelt when we need him? Where's the can-do, take-charge, full-speed-ahead spirit that once defined the American character? What's happened to our political will and civic enterprise, our vision and moral fortitude, our Yankee know-how and ingenuity, our ability and desire to tackle any problem, to take on any challenge, to do what needs to be done — with dispatch and care and pride?

There's nothing special about the Bowman Avenue Bridge — and that's the problem. This bridge is just another dismal example of a disease that's consuming the soul of America. For me, it's a maddening symbol, right in my own back yard, of the incompetence that is turning the United States into a second-rate nation and a Third World country.

> ▶ *In New Jersey, the State Commission of Investigation calls for drastic reforms to protect patients from drug-addicted, senile, mentally ill, or incompetent doctors. One case cited: an anesthesiologist who left a patient's side during an operation to have sex with a nurse in a closet. The patient died on the operating table.*

> ▶ *New York Telephone has to test 57,000 people before it can find 2100 qualified enough to become operators and repair technicians.*

> ▶ *Because of inadequate soil testing, a new interchange for the Schuylkill Expressway in Philadelphia begins to sink so badly that it must be torn down, redesigned, and rebuilt — a monumental bungle that may cost taxpayers $50 million.*

> ▶ *A Piedmont jetliner, with a hundred people on board, makes an emergency landing in Greensboro, North Car-*

olina, when its left landing gear cannot be lowered because it is jammed by a rubber wheel chock left behind by mechanics.

▸ *Because of a mistake made by a printing contractor, all 990 diplomas awarded to the midshipmen who graduated from the U.S. Naval Academy at Annapolis in 1990 include the line "The Seal of the Navel Academy is hereunto affixed."*

▸ *Encouraged by the Pentagon's lax oversight, military suppliers pad their bills by outrageous amounts, charging taxpayers $117 each for soap dish covers, $120 each for cup dispensers, $436 each for hammers, $641 each for porcelain urinals, $999 each for pliers, and $1868 each for toilet seat covers.*

What do I mean by incompetence? Strictly speaking, it refers to a lack of ability, but today, for many Americans, *incompetence* has become a catchword for a larger malaise. Simply stated, we have lost our purpose, our moral ambition, our sense of social obligation. In this broader light, incompetence is the failure to do what you ought to do, either because you can't or because you won't.

Incompetents come in two varieties: those who don't do what they should because they don't have the skill or training, and those who don't do what they should because they're lazy, sloppy, careless, and, frankly, don't give a damn. The United States has plenty of both types, at every level of society, among all kinds of people, in all sorts of vocations and professions.

Incompetence is the *Exxon Valdez* (cost: at least $2 billion for cleanup, incalculable damage to the environment), and mismanagement of the Energy Department's nuclear

weapons plants (cost: $150 billion), and a nation that contin-
ues to ring up tremendous budget deficits (an estimated $318
billion for fiscal 1991) and foreign trade imbalances (about
$100 billion for 1990).

Incompetence is the Philadelphia Police Department destroying a neighborhood by dropping a bomb on an occupied
row house to evict a bunch of obnoxious revolutionaries (cost:
eleven lives, sixty-one houses, at least $22.6 million), and a
doped-up Conrail engineer running a string of locomotives
into the path of an Amtrak passenger train (cost: 16 lives, 175
persons injured, millions of dollars in equipment and property
damage).

Incompetence is the high school graduate who can't read
or write or do simple arithmetic, the U.S. citizen who believes
that the Congress is appointed by the President, and the
ninety-four million Americans who don't know that their
own planet orbits the sun once a year.

Incompetence is the plumber who never shows, the
mail-order house that sends you the wrong merchandise, the
hospital accounting department that keeps badgering you with
computerized dunning notices for a bill you paid a year ago,
the sulky department store clerk who acts as if she's doing
you a favor by waiting on you, the empty-headed operator who
transfers your call to the wrong party, and the gum-popping
secretary who can't be bothered to help because she's too busy
chatting on the phone or carrying on with her cronies.

Incompetence is professors who plagiarize and scientists who fudge data. It's arrogant doctors who are too self-
important to return an anxious patient's telephone calls, and
greedy lawyers who make disputes so acrimonious that they
cost a fortune to settle.

Incompetence is too many college grads chasing MBAs
and BMWs, specializing in M&As and arranging LBOs, peddling junk bonds, shuffling paper assets, gutting companies,
creating nothing of value — but scoring high on their MBOs.

It's the self-promoting go-go biz whiz who runs the company into the ground and then brassily bails out with a million-dollar "golden parachute."

Incompetence is the Peter Principle and the art of failing upward. It's corporate facemen and hustlers and nice-guy managers who avoid conflict, straight talk, and tough decisions. It's insecure company despots who filter reality through obeisant yes men. It's myopic, risk-averse CEOs who starve R&D to fatten quarterly profits, and timid, passive boards of directors who rubber-stamp spectacular raises for top executives despite unspectacular, often paltry, accomplishment.

Incompetence is arrogant reporters who mangle the facts. It's *New Yorker* journalists who fabricate quotes and invent scenes to portray a "higher truth." It's newspapers that are so "reader friendly" and "customer driven" they've become glorified TV guides encapsulated in puff and fluff, trivia and ephemera. It's video hype and glitz and "infotainment" and TV news actors who know more about grooming their hair than reporting a story.

Incompetence is unsafe automobiles that have to be recalled, houses with warped floors and flimsy walls, particleboard furniture that's stapled together, and plastic components that break before the product's out of the box.

Incompetence is corporate and political leaders who, after a calamity, piously proclaim, "I take full responsibility" — and then don't. It's workers who say, "It's not my job"; "Why knock yourself out?"; "It's good enough"; "Nobody will see it"; "The customer will never know"; "It's the computer's fault"; "Just pack it and ship it." It's the *mañana* mentality and the urge, in the face of a difficult task, to whistle, along with Bobby McFerrin, "Don't Worry, Be Happy."

Incompetence is vanity and PR and people who talk about "massaging" or "positioning" or "spin control." It's a society that celebrates style over substance, image over reality, credentials over experience; a society that embraces the credo of the Philadelphia sheriff John Green — "Fake it till you make it"; a society devoted to consuming and acquiring, to self-fulfillment and self-indulgence, a society infatuated with money, power, sex, and drugs, a narcissistic, solipsistic, materialistic society saturated with advertising, dominated by entertainment, and living only for the here and now.

► *Thousands of pints of suspect blood and other blood components are released by blood banks and commercial plasma centers because of testing errors, computer problems, and other mistakes. Blood transfusions, often unnecessary, spread hepatitis to at least forty thousand people a year. Since 1981, more than twenty-six hundred patients have contracted AIDS through transfusions of infected blood.*

► *In New York City, an estimated twelve thousand babies were born addicted in 1989, and the number of children in foster care doubled from twenty-seven thousand in 1987 to more than fifty thousand, mainly because of parental drug abuse.*

► *A Northwest Airlines Boeing 727 with ninety-one passengers aboard lands safely in Minneapolis after a fifty-minute flight from Fargo, North Dakota, even though the plane's three pilots are apparently drunk. Less than ten hours before takeoff, the flight's captain consumed as many as twenty rum-and-Diet Cokes, and the first officer and flight engineer shared at least six pitchers of beer. All three pilots were fired and later convicted on federal charges of flying while intoxicated.*

► *The nation's fleet of B-2 Stealth bombers, expected to cost $70.2 billion, will need 120 air-conditioned garages*

*costing $1.6 billion because — among other reasons —
the cockpit windows don't open, and damaging heat
can't escape.*

▶ *In several places along a new interstate highway in suburban Philadelphia, contractors have poured weak concrete and defective support columns for overpasses. A
state engineer says one of the highway's bridges could
be unsafe and another could deteriorate early. Some
bridge columns are pocked with holes so deep that the
steel reinforcing bars are visible.*

▶ *The U.S. Occupational Safety and Health Administration proposes a record $6.1 million fine against USX
Corporation for two thousand safety violations at its
Fairless Works steel mill. During a recent two-year period, accidents at the Pennsylvania plant killed three
workers; one victim fell through a rusted platform and
into a vat of hot metal.*

Sometimes it's difficult to tell where incompetence ends
and outright fraud, greed, and corruption begin. The HUD
scandal (cost: $4 billion and counting) is about titanic inepti-
tude and mismanagement, but it's also about ostensibly
respectable people becoming poverty pimps, lining their
pockets by subverting housing programs intended to help the
poor. The savings and loan scandal is about gross stupidity
and shortsightedness, but it's also about avaricious bankers
pumping up profits by making reckless, high-risk loans, secure in the knowledge that ultimately taxpayers will foot the
bill. (And some bill it is. Estimates of the cost of the bailout
range from $500 billion [the General Accounting Office] to
$1.4 trillion [Stanford economist Dan Brumbaugh]. At a mere
$500 billion, the bailout will cost the American people more

than all of World War II did. Or, to put it another way, it will cost every family in the United States $30 every month for the next thirty years!)

There is, admittedly, no way to quantify a nation's incompetence and to prove that more of it exists today than, say, thirty or forty years ago. But there is a growing perception that things don't work the way they used to, that other people can't be counted on anymore — to be responsible, to show up, to do what they promised, to perform a job well.

Amitai Etzioni, a professor of sociology at George Washington University, told me: "Our society is coming apart, because incompetence is practically all-pervasive. We've lost our sense of discipline, integrity, and devotion to diligent effort. We've become too permissive and laissez-faire.

"It's most apparent in the routine functions of life. Look at the next ten people you have appointments with — no one comes on time anymore. You almost don't expect it. There's no uptightness left — a quality you can see in the societies we admire, the Germans and the Japanese. Those are nations where the trains run on time, where commitments are rock solid, where the population is infused with a sense of conscientiousness."

E. Digby Baltzell, a retired University of Pennsylvania sociologist, echoed Etzioni's sentiments: "It's awful. The incompetence is just vast." When I visited his town house in Center City Philadelphia, he invited me up to his second-floor study. From a file cabinet in the corner, he pulled out a bulging folder entitled THINGS DON'T WORK and, in a voice thick with disgust, began reading headlines from newspaper clippings he'd saved: Philadelphia Electric nuclear plant closed, operators found asleep. Thirty-three percent of MX missiles unusable, accuracy in doubt. Amtrak train was speeding, investigators say. Accidents increase on U.S. airlines.

"It's epidemic all over — in schools, in universities,

down at NASA, the airlines, public agencies, the government," Baltzell said. "We're aspiring downward, not upward."

Another Penn professor I talked to, Vukan R. Vuchic, is an expert on transportation systems and technology. He sees an America riddled with incompetence, an America in industrial retreat, an America that has virtually given up, for example, manufacturing electric transit vehicles, such as subways and light-rail trains. "We're talking about a business worth more than a million dollars a day. And we're giving all that money to foreign producers, the Canadians, the Japanese, the French, the Italians.

"If you compare our performance, our efficiency, our quality of life with some other countries, we're losing tremendously. The quality of public services has been so low for so long that people have low expectations. There is too much tolerance and a sloppy, anything-goes attitude. The result is that poor performance that would cause a scandal elsewhere is taken as routine here. And once it's accepted as routine, the people who are performing their jobs poorly know they can get away with it."

"If our society weren't benefiting from a reverse brain drain, if we weren't able to attract competence from outside this country," says Paul R. Kleindorfer, a professor of decision sciences and economics at Penn's Wharton School, "we'd be dead in the water."

At a dinner party in Austin, I complained about American incompetence to Walt Rostow, a former adviser to Lyndon Johnson and a professor of political economics at the University of Texas. "The rest of the world is laughing at us," Rostow told me. "We're like a giant who can't pull his pants up."

▶ *The U.S. Department of Education estimates that twenty-three million adults over the age of eighteen — or about 9 percent of Americans — are functionally illiterate and incapable of performing any but the most menial tasks. An additional forty-six million adults — or another 18 percent of the population — are considered to be just marginally literate.*

▶ *The U.S. Army says more than a quarter of its enlistees cannot read training manuals written at the seventh-grade level.*

▶ *The Public Citizen Health Research Group, founded by Ralph Nader, says unnecessary and incompetent care contributes to the deaths of more than 200,000 Americans a year.*

▶ *The Army's new $14 million Apache attack helicopter cannot be flown in the rain, pilots tell congressional investigators. Nearly half the McDonnell Douglas helicopters have problems before they take off, and once they're running, something goes wrong an average of every fifty-four minutes. An Apache devours spare parts so fast it costs $5700 an hour — nearly $100 a minute — to keep it flying. During a five-day war game, all twelve Apaches in one Army unit failed; rotor blades splintered, cannons jammed, and when the cannons worked, they shook so violently that they shut down the Apaches' electronic target finders. During the Panama invasion, the hot, humid air and water generated by the air conditioning, required to keep the Apaches' high-tech equipment running, shorted out the aircraft's electronics — which Army mechanics scrambled to dry out in ovens.*

▶ *Four people die and 165 are hospitalized when a subway train derails in Philadelphia after a switch is*

*thrown by a dragging traction motor that maintenance
workers bolted on improperly.*

▶ *A twelve-inch Exxon pipeline ruptures under the Arthur
Kill Waterway, which separates Staten Island and New
Jersey. A leak-detection alarm flashes, but employees
don't take it seriously for nearly six hours, because the
alarm is known to be defective. Result: 567,000 gallons
of heating oil foul surrounding wetlands.*

Thirty years or so ago, when I was a boy on the shy side
of ten, I spent most of my allowance money at a five-and-ten
called Mapes in the nearby village of Narberth. Mapes was a
funky, tumbledown establishment with creaky wood floors
and paint peeling off the walls, but we kids loved it because its
toy department was stocked with all manner of gaudy junk
that usually cost less than a dollar. I remember particularly
the friction-motor cars and trucks that were made of recycled
food cans whose original labels we could see on the inside.

Like almost everything in Mapes's toy department,
these homely, laughable vehicles were labeled MADE IN
JAPAN — which back then meant cheap, flimsy, and inferior.
Those were the days when almost everything Japan produced
was cheap, flimsy, and inferior. But that did not last long.
Struggling frantically to resuscitate an economy flattened by
World War II, the Japanese eagerly copied the ingenious manufacturing and marketing techniques of their American con-
querors, elevating to the level of a god the statistician W.
Edwards Deming, who emphasized quality control above all.
Meanwhile, American businessmen, cocky and complacent,
rewarded themselves with handsome bonuses, bought labor
peace with generous wage boosts, and in general spent more
effort improving their golf handicap than addressing the challenges of the future. We were still inventing things and manufacturing things, of course, but we were paying far too little

attention to quality and long-term investment in plant and equipment and far too much attention to quantity, quarterly dividends, and yearly profits. By the time we woke up, we discovered that the Japanese had seized the lead or were posing a serious threat in such essential — and at one time seemingly impregnable — American industries as steelmaking, automobile manufacturing, and electronics.

It's a measure of how competent we once were and how incompetent we've since become that MADE IN JAPAN is now synonymous with innovation, cleverness, high quality, and technological wizardry, while MADE IN THE U.S.A. — despite the patriotic appeals of American labor unions — has lost much of its cachet. Japanese products are so obviously superior and usually such a good value (I am writing this on a Japanese Epson computer, which I chose over a similar, and more expensive, American IBM model) that it's little wonder many Americans — their loyalty to their homeland notwithstanding — are buying Hondas and Toyotas, Sonys and Panasonics, and the Japanese own Rockefeller Center and half of Hollywood.

Not surprisingly, Japan no longer feels nor shows the same respect toward the nation that was once its mentor. That's the message that comes through loud and clear in *The Japan That Can Say No*, a controversial book that was originally written by Sony chairman Akio Morita and Shintaro Ishihara, an outspoken intellectual and right-wing member of the Japanese Diet. (The book sold more than a million copies in Japan and has since been published in the United States. But the English-language edition carries only Ishihara's name, since Morita refused to allow his essays to be included.)

In the original Japanese edition, Morita and Ishihara portray a United States that's on the skids "because of economic self-indulgence, indiscipline, and executive greed." They depict a nation that's become lazy and soft, its strength sapped by racial conflict and an inferior system of education. They

describe a fading superpower beset by false pride, bad management, arrogance, and terminal incompetence.

Japan has plenty of its own problems and is far from perfect, but much of what Morita and Ishihara say is true. Every
day, I see distressing confirmation of their criticism and glar-
ing evidence of America's decline. In fact, I'm confronted with
it nearly every time I try to run an errand or drive into the city.
For there, blocking my way, is the Bowman Avenue Bridge,
overgrown with weeds, still barricaded. It is more than just a
pain in the neck. It is more than just a construction project
that seems forever on hold. It is a monument to bureaucratic
bungling, to paralysis through analysis, to an effete techno-
cracy more skillful at meeting and dealing than making and
doing. As such, the Bowman Avenue Bridge is also a warning
sign: that we've lost our grit and resolve, that we've become
sluggish and diffident in the face of problems and challenges,
that we aren't working as hard as we must and the work we're
producing is too often slipshod and unacceptable, that indeed
our greatness is in jeopardy because we've become — far
faster than many of us realize and would like to admit — the
United States of Incompetence.

2 "The Center Cannot Hold"

It is a very serious fact that nowadays no one in our country is acquiring faithfully the carpenter's trade. Much of this lamentable condition of things is no doubt due to the fact that machine work has supplanted the handwork of former times. Doors, blinds, sashes, mouldings are now turned out by the cord and mile, and all done in such greedy haste, and with the greenest of lumber, that if it does not tumble to pieces in transportation it is sure to do so very soon after entering into the house structure. Nevertheless, the miserable truth yet remains that any man who has nailed up a few boxes, or stood in front of a circular saw for a few months, feels competent to exercise all the duties of that most honorable craft — the building of a house.

THE PASSAGE above sounds like yet another indictment of the shoddiness of today's workmanship. But this criticism of the quality of American carpentry was written more than a century ago, in 1886, by Edward Sylvester Morse, an American zoologist and inventor, in his book *Japanese Homes and Their Surroundings*.

Reading it raises two important questions. Is incompetence truly sweeping the land today? If so, is it really worse than before?

Many experts and social critics say no way. The whole

idea is pure poppycock. Stop romanticizing the past. Things have never been better. More Americans are working than ever before, and many of us are working as hard and as long as the work-addicted Japanese. We're still launching businesses, scoring scientific breakthroughs, dreaming up inventions, developing new products, erecting skyscrapers, writing good books, and making movies that the entire world loves. (Even American cars are beginning to look and work better.) In fact, now that the Cold War is over, we may be on the brink of a golden age of unparalleled achievement, justice, and prosperity. The rest of the world still looks to our democratic government and capitalistic economy as a model; witness the transformation of the Soviet Union. Besides, they say, incompetence is all a matter of definition, all a matter of perspective. And who's to judge?

"In an industrial, highly technological society," says the historian Henry Steele Commager of Amherst, "everything is more complicated, so there are more chances for things to go wrong."

"I don't see any massive rise in incompetence," says Arnold Packer, a senior research fellow at the Hudson Institute. "There have always been plenty of people who did their jobs poorly, and there's never been a shortage of lousy products."

"You have to have a certain amount of compassion for America," says Edwin Mansfield, director of the Center for Economics and Technology at the University of Pennsylvania. "Much of what looks like incompetence today is not so much incompetence as a reflection of the fact that the ball game's changed."

Larry Hirschhorn, a consultant with the Wharton Center for Applied Research, says, "Incompetence is more conspicuous, because we can't afford to waste as much as we used to. In the old days, it didn't matter how efficient we were because there was this limitless expanse of territory and resources."

"It's not so much that individual people don't care," says Ross A. Webber, a professor of management at the Wharton School, "as that the technology that has grown out of the desire to save on labor expenses has made everything inhuman."

"Incompetence seems to reflect on a person's character. It implies a moral deficiency; it implies inferior human material," says the city planner Edmund N. Bacon. "When you use the word *incompetence,* aren't you really talking about alienation?"

Decrying incompetence is simply a semantic ruse, others contend. It's just another way of rephrasing the same old declinist argument — an argument at least as ancient as the 4800-year-old Assyrian tablet that lamented: "The earth is degenerating these days. Bribery and corruption abound. Children no longer mind their parents. Every man wants to write a book, and it is evident that the end of the world is approaching."

Obviously, the United States is not about to collapse. And obviously we are still ahead of the rest of the world in many, many respects. And yes, we have made great progress technologically. And yes, some of the products we manufacture are better and more reliable than ever before. And yes, incompetence has always existed, things are more complicated, the ball game's changed, our resources are more limited, and the question of incompetence is, to a large extent, a matter of perspective.

But these are basically excuses, rationalizations for substandard performance. As such, they are less and less supportable at a time when technology, to a terrific degree, has magnified the consequences of incompetence. (An incompetent Amtrak engineer can endanger many more lives than the incompetent driver of a horse-drawn coach; an incompetent control-room technician at a nuclear power plant can wreak much more havoc than the incompetent operator of a water-powered nineteenth-century mill.) Furthermore, just because incompetence implies decline and just because declinist arguments have been made before doesn't mean they're bunkum. In fact, it's precisely because such arguments have a long pedigree that we should heed them. For declinists often have good reason to fulminate. Nations *do* rise and fall. Civilizations *do* begin and end. "Of the twenty-three great civilizations, twenty-one died without ever a shot being fired — they died from within," the British historian Arnold Toynbee once remarked. In the life of a nation, there is no neutral ground between growth and decay; we are always doing one or the other. Which is it now? There's no doubt in my mind. But for all those who believe incompetence isn't really a problem, for all those who think most everything is hunky-dory and the United States is doing swell, let me raise a few questions:

If we're so competent, how come so many of us are ignorant savages and how come so many of our schools stink and how come so many of our cities are squalid slums?

If we're so competent, how come we keep hocking the future, spending hundreds of billions more than we take in year after year?

If we're so competent, how come we persist in electing a bunch of clowns, sending them to the Big Top in Washington, where, in 1990, their farcical bickering over the federal budget dragged on so long that the government ran out of money and had to shut down?

If we're so competent, how come so many people abroad — and a good many Americans — turn up their noses at the products we make?

If we're so competent, how come, fifteen years ago, we were the only producer of semiconductor memory chips for computers, and today the Japanese make more than 75 percent of the world total?

If we're so competent, how come, as recently as 1981, we

were the world's leading maker of machine tools, and today we're in third place, behind Japan and West Germany?

If we're so competent, how come our share of the world consumer electronics market has shrunk since the 1970s from 70 percent to 5 percent?

If we're so competent, how come, ten years ago, we made 88 percent of the telephones in this country, and now we make under 25 percent; how come we made 60 percent of the color TVs, and now we make only 10 percent; how come we made 10 percent of the tape recorders, and now we make none — not a single one (and we invented all these items!)?

Yes, the question of incompetence *is* a matter of perspective, and you don't have to be a pessimist to see plainly that, in many important ways, America is slipping — and slipping badly.

As recently as 1983, we were the world's largest creditor nation; we are now the world's largest debtor nation. In 1989, our net debt — the difference between what Americans own overseas and what foreigners own in the United States — was nearly $664 billion. That's 25 percent more than in the previous year, and many economists believe that by the mid-nineties the figure will top $1 trillion.

In 1980, the national debt — what we taxpayers and our successors collectively owe for all the money Uncle Sam has borrowed over the years to finance our accumulated federal budget deficits — was under $1 trillion. Now, it has more than tripled to over $3 trillion. It took more than two hundred years to pile up the first trillion in debt, but in only a decade we've added two trillion more. In the 1970s, one of every twelve tax dollars sent to Washington went directly for interest on the federal debt; today, debt service takes one of every six tax dollars.

In 1989, our gross national product — the total value of our annual output of goods and services — was $5.2 trillion, still robust and tops in the world, but not by the margin it once was. Some economists predict that early in the next century, the Japanese, whose 1989 GNP of $2.8 trillion was just over half as large as ours, will actually overtake us in economic output. In productivity growth, the United States is squandering its once-commanding lead. Our productivity now is just 30 percent greater than that of other industrialized nations; in 1972, we were cruising with an 87 percent advantage. In Japan, the average worker has more than doubled productivity over the past eighteen years. Little wonder: since 1988, Japanese businessmen have devoted about 60 percent of their capital investment to research and development and the creation of new processes of design and manufacture. In 1989, for the first time since World War II, Japan spent more money than the United States on new factories and equipment. Specifically, Japanese investment jumped to a record 23.6 percent of the nation's gross domestic product, exceeding U.S. investment by $36 billion, even though the U.S. economy is twice as large as Japan's. "America is looking like an aging athlete," says Kent Hughes, president of the Council on Competitiveness, a group of business leaders, union officials, and academics concerned about America's position in the world. "Still on top but trying to ignore all the younger talent that is breaking into the line-up."

American manufacturers talk constantly about quality and boast about it in advertising, but for years now we have been lagging behind Japan and West Germany when it comes, for instance, to producing automobiles free of defects. J. D. Power and Associates, a California-based automotive marketing and research firm, compiles quality ratings for cars based on the number of problems encountered in the first ninety days of ownership. To the automobile industry, the Power quality ratings are the equivalent of Hollywood's Academy Awards. Its quality survey of 1990 models included only one American car — General Motors' Buick, which placed fifth.

All the other cars with high quality ratings were manufactured by either Japanese or West German automakers.

America once had a standard of living — defined as real gross domestic product per capita — that was the envy of the world. But it has begun to slide. For several years now, we've been trailing West Germany; and other industrialized countries, such as Canada, France, Great Britain, Italy, and Japan, are rapidly narrowing the gap. What this means is that the citizens of those countries may soon enjoy higher incomes and more economic choices than we Americans. In 1987, for instance, average American manufacturing workers were earning barely $1000 more in salary and benefits in real terms than they were in 1972, while average Japanese workers were earning about $5000 more and average West German workers about $7500 more.

Already, the effects are being felt. Many young Americans live with their parents after college and into their thirties, or they still rent apartments after the arrival of children because they can't afford to purchase a home. In many families, both husband and wife must work, sometimes at more than one job, to meet staggering monthly mortgage payments and to achieve the same middle-class comforts they took for granted when they were growing up.

The United States has some of the world's best doctors and hospitals, and we spend $650 billion a year on health care. Many citizens do receive superb medical treatment, but a lot of others — mostly poor women and children and the unemployed — do not. About fifty million Americans — one fifth of our population — have inadequate health insurance, and as many as 37 million have none at all. The United States has an infant mortality rate that puts us in twenty-first place among developed nations. What this means is that babies are more likely to die before their first birthday here than in twenty other countries. The infant death rate in the nation's capital, and in Detroit and Baltimore, is shamefully close to that of a Third World country. Life expectancy for the average American today is seventy-five years, a figure that ranks us sixteenth among the world's industrialized nations. In other words, we can expect to have shorter lives, on average, than the citizens of many other Western countries.

According to a recent study, a boy born in Harlem today is likely to die earlier than a boy born in Bangladesh. Between 1978 and 1988, the number of babies born with syphilis increased sevenfold. In a recent report, the Senate Judiciary Committee estimated that one in every hundred Americans — or about 2.2 million citizens — is a hard-core cocaine addict. About 100,000 babies born each year may be permanently handicapped because of their mothers' use of crack cocaine during pregnancy.

In a nation where image-conscious corporations spend $850,000 for each thirty-second television commercial during the Super Bowl, in a nation with more than sixty billionaires and scores of multimillionaire football, basketball, and baseball players, in a nation that each year throws away enough aluminum to rebuild our air fleet seventy-one times, enough steel to reconstruct Manhattan, and enough wood and paper to heat five million homes for two hundred years, more than half a million Americans are homeless, including at least 100,000 children.

The Fordham Institute for Innovation in Social Policy publishes what it calls an Index of Social Health, a measurement of the nation's progress, or lack thereof, in addressing seventeen major social problems: infant mortality, child abuse, poverty among children, suicide among teenagers, drug abuse, high school drop-outs, unemployment, poverty among heads of households, the health insurance gap, the unemployment insurance gap, poverty among those over sixty-five, out-of-pocket health costs for those over sixty-five, homicides, highway deaths caused by intoxication, the food stamp gap, the gap between the rich and poor, and the lack of affordable housing. The index charts the nation's performance since 1970 on a scale running from 0 to 100, with 100 representing not some unattainable ideal but our best recorded achievement in dealing with a particular problem during the period of study.

In 1987, the most recent year examined, the Index of Social Health remained at its lowest point — 35 — *for the second consecutive year.* Eight of the seventeen social problems plunged to their worst level ever, including child abuse, teenage suicide, and the gap between rich and poor. In 1970, the index stood at 68. "The worsening trend, both in the overall index and in specific problems, is cause for concern," says Marc L. Miringoff, the institute's director. "Particularly striking is the steady, almost uninterrupted decline of the index as a whole and the large number of problems reaching their worst level."

As a kind of Dow Jones Average of social pathology, the Fordham index is an extremely useful tool. But the problems it dramatically quantifies and reduces to depressing bar graphs should be apparent to any reasonably sentient and informed citizen. They are problems that are obvious, and obviously getting worse, all across America, but particularly in our cities, some of which are becoming downright uninhabitable. This is a tragic and frightening development, for great cities are the salt marshes of civilization; for all their smells and muck, cities remain the source of ideas, talents, and movements that lift the human condition.

But consider the abysmal state of America's large cities today, especially in the Northeast and Midwest. Philadelphia, the city where I work, is practically bankrupt and presents aspects reminiscent of Beirut, Calcutta, or war-ravaged Dresden. Crack dealers rule certain battered neighborhoods, cruising imperiously in flashy Jeep Cherokees with tinted windows and booming stereos, and enforcing their dominion with high-caliber semiautomatic weapons. In 1990, there were a record 525 homicides in Philadelphia. The police are exhausted, the courts are hopelessly backed up, the prisons are explosively overcrowded. So overwhelmed is the "criminal justice system" by the onslaught of violent crime that property crime has, in effect, been legalized. Whole blocks of row houses are abandoned and crumbling. Impoverished citizens sleep in cardboard boxes or on sidewalk steam vents. It is impossible to walk through Center City without being accosted by a beggar, who often wears the demented look of a drug addict.

Many middle-class residents are fleeing the city because they are tired of steep taxes and meager city services. They are tired of the trash and filth and the stench of urine, tired of being mugged and panhandled, tired of having their cars vandalized or stolen, tired of having their houses burglarized or sprayed with graffiti, tired of waking up to find drug syringes or crack vials on their porches, or their plants and shrubs dug out by thieves, tired of supporting lousy public schools and paying the highest car insurance rates in the country.

Indeed, there's a desperate sense that the barbarians have taken over, that a hostile and antisocial underclass is proliferating uncontrollably. Many Philadelphians feel besieged, and after many years of contributing time and know-how and energy to the city, sacrificing for the city and tolerating the city's many vexations, some of the diehard urbanites, the optimistic liberals devoted to racial harmony and ethnic and cultural diversity, are flocking to the bland and bourgeois suburbs.

Tragically, these are the very people the city can least afford to lose. Even more tragically, the plight of Philadelphia is not unique. To a greater or lesser degree, the same problems plague other major cities in America, and to the extent that cities are places where social ills are concentrated and hence magnified, the perilous state of Philadelphia is but an early reflection of the perilous state of the nation.

Admittedly, Philadelphia's troubles have been exacerbated by monstrous incompetence and a titanic lack of leadership. The mayor, W. Wilson Goode, is energetic but inept; the City Council is a laughingstock. Nevertheless, a scan of the national horizon isn't exactly reassuring. Consider our contemporary heroes. We have meretricious celebrities galore. But heroes? How about our country's recent Presidents? Johnson, Nixon, Ford, Carter, and Reagan? Is your skin puckering into patriotic goose bumps? Or are you still wondering how this mighty nation could spawn such a pathetic cavalcade of scoundrels and bumblers?

In the last presidential race competence was an issue, perhaps *the* issue. In fact, Michael "Coming to America" Dukakis, the Democratic candidate, said as much. "This election is about competence, not about ideology," he solemnly declared. Those of us disgusted with glamour-boy politicians who are all show and no go were encouraged and hopeful; at last, a hands-on, nuts-and-bolts, detail-oriented kind of guy who would bring order, reason, and discipline to government, along with sophisticated management skills. But, alas, Dukakis and his earnest band quickly demonstrated *their* competence by squandering a seventeen-point postconvention lead in the polls and blowing the election.

Of course, it hardly helped that Dukakis, for all his bright ideas and good intentions, has the warmth, geniality, and charisma of a dead haddock — a fatal form of incompetence in a politician who aspires to the presidency, a job, after all, that requires some measure of rapport with The People. Then again, what if he had won? After returning to Boston, Dukakis watched his unfavorable rating climb to an incredible 79 percent as his much-vaunted "Massachusetts miracle" evaporated, the state's budget deficit swelled to over three quarters of a billion dollars, and its bond rating sank to the lowest in the nation.

The man who beat Dukakis was George "I Coulda Been a Country Club Steward" Bush, the affable Yalie prepster who has made a career out of playing second banana. I didn't vote for Bush, but when he was nominated at the Republican convention in the New Orleans Superdome, he gave what I thought was an inspiring acceptance speech. I was even hopeful that he'd surprise me by becoming a bold leader who would make good on his promise to turn America into a "kinder, gentler" nation. (I had my doubts, to be sure. After all, this is the man who stunned me, and the rest of the nation, by naming J. Danforth Quayle, an obscure Indiana senator, as his running mate. Whatever possessed Bush to anoint such a lightweight and second-rater? Blond, bland, telegenic, and eminently unencumbered by brilliance, Quayle has since become a national poster boy for mediocrity and incompetence.)

Bush's first year and a half in office was less than enthralling. He distinguished himself mainly by exhibiting the manic, aggressively agreeable personality of a television game-show host, standing tall for the status quo and, let us not forget, parading the troops in Panama. Some may argue that deploying 22,500 soldiers to nab the drug thug Manuel Noriega was a bit heavy-handed. Maybe it's true, as one editorial writer noted, that this mission could have been accomplished by the Butte, Montana, police department. On the other hand, in light of American military adventures up till then (Vietnam, the 1975 attempt to liberate the crew of the *Mayaguez*, the aborted 1980 raid to free the American embassy hostages in Iran, the 1983 slaughter of 241 Marines by a terrorist bomb in Beirut, the 1983 invasion of the Caribbean island of Grenada, the loss of 37 sailors in the 1987 attack on the USS *Stark*, the shooting down of an Iranian airliner by the USS *Vincennes* in 1988), it was probably a prudent move. It certainly reduced the chances of an American rout.

Fortunately, Noriega was vanquished, and Bush puffed out his chest, confident he'd proven that he isn't a wimp. Meanwhile, however, he was paying only lip service to problems and challenges at home. "Self-satisfied and reactive," *Time* magazine called him, adding: "His long-term goals, beyond hoping for a kinder, gentler nation, have been lost in a miasma of public relations stunts." By the summer of 1990, with the nation slipping into a recession and Congress tangling, with escalating rancor and futility, over the budget mess, the United States seemed utterly rudderless and impotent, and the country's mood was dark and pessimistic.

Then, to make matters worse, in early August, Saddam Hussein, the brutal ruler of Iraq, invaded neighboring Kuwait. Hussein was gambling that no one would stand up to him, particularly the soft and sybaritic United States, which lately had seemed all bark and no bite. But Hussein miscalculated. Whether motivated by machismo, oil, or a genuine desire to establish a "new world order," Bush promptly took offense, telling the Butcher of Baghdad, in effect: Get out or I'll throw you out. With skill and speed, he assembled a coalition of allies, won the backing of the United Nations, and sent more than half a million American troops to the Persian Gulf to "kick butt." They did so, of course, with astonishing success.

Admittedly, Iraq is hardly a superpower, Saddam Hussein wasn't exactly a master strategist, and his fearsome Republican Guard, it turns out, was a tad overrated. But whether you thought the war foolish or wise, there was no denying that George Bush emerged, at last, as a leader — decisive, resolute, capable of exercising power, enforcing his will, and realizing his moral vision. In the triumphal afterglow of Operation Desert Storm, grateful citizens awarded him approval ratings that reached a saintly 90 percent. And as yellow ribbons and flags proliferated across the land, so too did a welcome spirit of old-fashioned patriotism, and with it the optimistic hope that perhaps it wasn't too late, that perhaps America could still muster the mettle to stem the slow rot at home.

It is a hope Bush has shrewdly tried to encourage, for he realizes that he faces plenty of other battles on other fronts, and there are serious doubts whether he — or anyone else in Washington, for that matter — is concerned or competent enough to join those battles, let alone win them. Now that the troops are home and the celebratory parades and fireworks are over, it's business as usual in Washington, where both parties have perfected the politics of self-interest and shortsighted-ness. For all his bravura abroad, Bush has been aggravatingly reticent about addressing the nation's domestic woes. As for Congress, it continues to hone its specialty: ducking or skirt-ing major issues and problems. Capitol Hill is scarcely differ-ent from the loathsome morass that prompted *Time* to wonder, more than a year before the war, "Is Government Dead?" It is still a place paralyzed by a "neurosis of accepted limits"; it is still a place swarming with "weakness, egotism, venality, and sheer political cowardice."

Government incompetence has always been something of a tautology. But it has become so chronic and overwhelm-ing that our political system seems to be degenerating from a democracy into a kakistocracy — government by the worst. Running for national office is now such an ordeal that anyone who seriously aspires to it must be certifiably insane. Most of us inhabit this planet for only seventy or eighty years, so who in his right mind wants to spend a precious year or two, even a few months, enduring the silliness and humiliation of the modern political campaign: the endless round of dining on rubber chickens, kissing frightened babies, wearing funny hats, mugging for photographers, making empty speeches to catatonic audiences? Men of the depth and stature and princi-ple of Thomas Jefferson and Abraham Lincoln would fail mis-erably in this age of sound bites and spin doctors. How would they handle the army of underemployed political reporters, eager to hype the most sordid shred of personal gossip into front-page news? How would they deal with the special-interest maniacs? The gun nuts? The pro-abortionists? The anti-abortionists? The flag wavers? The flag burners? How would they raise the millions of dollars necessary to mount an effective media campaign? From what political action committees and sleazy lobbyists would they stoop to beg money? And just how completely would they prostitute their integrity to get elected? After making all the promises necessary to seduce as many voters as possible, would they have any character left worth electing? Or would they wind up like so many of the yahoos and peckerwoods who now fill seats in the U.S. Congress — glib, feckless megalomaniacs with about as much moral fiber as a bowl of soggy corn flakes, gutless narcissists with blow-dried hair who have to take a poll every time they go to the bathroom.

Stuck with such a contemptible collection of blowhards and weasels, we voters don't have much of a choice. Or do we? Perhaps our politicians behave the way they do because there's no other way to get elected and keep the job. Forced to be inoffensive to win our votes, they offend us by their very inoffensiveness. Perhaps our public officials are merely exaggerated reflections of us, the people they represent. If they are conspicuously incompetent, perhaps the blame (some of it, anyway) lies with us, or at least the dwindling number of us who bother to vote. (In the 1990 midterm elections, the 36.4 percent turnout rate among eligible adults tied 1986 as the second lowest since 1942.)

When George Bush pledged to reduce the budget deficit and then urged us to read his lips, NO NEW TAXES, did we really believe him? Of course not. Any citizen with the intelligence of an eggplant knows, in his heart of hearts, that there's no way the United States can significantly cut the budget deficit without increasing revenues; that is, raising taxes. But the voters of America listened to Bush's fatuous promise and, in a burst of wish fulfillment, bought it. Relieved and grateful, we rewarded Bush by electing him President, just as, four years earlier, we punished Walter Mondale for having the temerity to be honest and tell us he *would* raise taxes.

Yes, Washington is crawling with phonies and incompetents, and they are there because we put them there, and the way they got our vote was largely by telling us what we wanted to hear. And what we still want to hear is that everything's copacetic, that Uncle Sam has a solution for every problem, that the government's job is to remove the risk from life, to provide gain without pain, and to do all that *right now*.

In a widely quoted speech delivered in the summer of 1989 at the National Press Club, Richard G. Darman, the director of the Office of Management and Budget, blasted both the government and the voters for acting like the spoiled child in the Maypo commercial who wants his cereal NOW! He labeled the phenomenon "Now-now-ism." Admittedly, Darman's credentials as a social critic are suspect, considering that he gets paid to massage the deficit numbers so that his boss, George Bush, looks good. Nevertheless, he talks a good game and — most amazing for a Washington politician — the words he used that day were his own: "The deficit is but one more symptom of our Now-now-ism . . . a kind of silent Now-now scream. It is the mathematical representation of our wish to buy now, pay later — or, more accurately, buy now and let others pay later . . . Collectively, we are engaged in a massive Backward Robin Hood transaction — robbing the future to give to the present . . ."

"The great 1960s and early 1970s metaphor for expanding human possibility was moonwalking, escaping earthly bonds, leaping to the moon. This captured the imagination and excitement of a generation. In the 1980s, 'moonwalking' has become an equally attractive excitement. But its meaning has changed. The moonwalking of the 1980s is an earthbound dance . . . a set of steps that give the appearance of forward movement, when they are really a backward slide."

On May 25, 1961, President John F. Kennedy stood before Congress and outlined a dream for the American people: "I believe that this nation should commit itself to achieving the goal, before this decade is out, of landing a man on the moon and returning him safely to Earth." It was an exciting, breathtaking challenge made during an exciting, breathtaking time, when America was full of itself, riding the crest of postwar prosperity, confident of its ability to solve any problem, win any war, develop the technology and competence to explore the New Frontier, and master the universe.

On July 20, 1969, we met Kennedy's challenge when Neil Armstrong set foot on the moon, 250,801 miles distant from Planet Earth. Armstrong proclaimed, "That's one step for a man, one giant leap for mankind," and all of us agreed with him. It was the climax of history's most difficult feat. And we Americans had done it! If we put our minds to it, we could do almost anything.

On January 28, 1986, the space shuttle *Challenger* exploded seventy-three seconds after blastoff, killing all seven of its crew members. Millions of people in the United States and around the world witnessed the disaster on television. The nation was shocked and horrified; men wept, women embraced in grief. It seemed like some surrealistic nightmare; for days people reeled in disbelief.

The accident happened because extremely cold weather on the morning of the launch froze the rubber O-rings, which were supposed to seal the joints of the solid-fuel booster rocket. Blazing-hot gases spurted from one of the joints and ignited the rocket's external fuel tank.

Later, a presidential commission revealed that NASA had known for years that the booster joints were faulty. In twenty-four previous shuttle flights, NASA had recorded forty-two instances of O-ring damage. Still, NASA deemed the problematic joints an acceptable risk, even though in 1982 the O-rings had been classified a "criticality 1," meaning that their failure could result in the loss of vehicle and crew.

On the eve of the *Challenger* flight, engineers from Morton Thiokol, the company that built the rocket booster, were so concerned about how the O-rings would perform in frigid temperatures that they urged NASA to postpone the launch. But NASA officials, eager to adhere to an overambitious flight schedule, disregarded the warning, and the next day the whole world saw the gruesome consequence of the agency's imprudence. Reacting to this spectacular example of incompetence, Senator John Glenn, of Ohio, who in 1962 had become the first American to orbit the Earth, said, "The mindset of a few people in key positions at NASA had changed from an optimistic, super-safety-conscious 'can-do' attitude . . . to an arrogant 'can't-fail' attitude."

To me, the history of the space program is a potent metaphor — a metaphor for how high we once soared and how low we've since plummeted. After the *Challenger* disaster, NASA drifted, demoralized and listless. Then, as *Voyager* 2 completed its twelve-year, 4.5-billion-mile flyby of the outer solar system in 1989, the agency began to perk up. For a while, space shuttles were winging into the sky again. With great fanfare, President Bush talked of establishing a working space station and sending man to Mars. It seemed, for a time, that at last NASA had struggled out of its despondency and overcome its inertia.

Then came the Hubble Space Telescope. When it was launched on April 24, 1990 — seven years late and more than $700 million over budget — it seemed that the United States would finally enjoy another triumph in space. The telescope was hailed as an exciting breakthrough that would revolutionize our understanding of the universe. Hubble would provide sharp, crystal-clear views of the heavens, undistorted by the Earth's atmosphere. Astronomers and scientists waited eagerly for what they hoped would be dramatic high-resolution pictures of cosmic phenomena unlike any seen from an observatory.

The pictures never came. Instead, the space telescope sent back blurry images that looked as if we were peering at the cosmos through eyes clouded by cataracts. Eventually, after all sorts of desperate remote-control manipulations, the awful truth could no longer be denied: the $1.5 billion Hubble Space Telescope would never function the way it was intended to because of a defect in a mirror that wasn't much more complicated than the one in the first telescope, fashioned by Galileo in 1609.

What should have been a redeeming victory for our space program turned into another humiliating disaster — and yet another striking example of American incompetence. The Harvard astronomer Clifford Stoll called the Hubble snafu "one of the worst things to happen to astronomy since the pope strung up Galileo." John Pike of the Federation of American Scientists lamented, "It's clear Murphy's law doesn't stop where space begins." And a fuming Senator Albert Gore, Jr., declared, "We owe it to the taxpayers to find out what went wrong, how to fix it, and make sure it never happens again."

Technically, the mirror was unable to focus because of a "spherical aberration." According to the NASA committee that investigated the Hubble fiasco, the problem was caused by a mistake in the template used to guide the grinding and polishing processes. Technicians at the Perkin-Elmer Corporation, the company that manufactured the mirror, were so confident the template was perfect that they ignored indications the mirror was flawed. (The same company, by the way, gave one of its subcontractors *backward* blueprints for Hubble guidance parts.) The defect could have been spotted, some experts said, if NASA's quality-control staff had tested the mirror thoroughly before the telescope was rocketed aloft. Instead, NASA's oversight of the contractors laboring on this high-profile, high-prestige project was positively lackadaisical. NASA accepted Perkin-Elmer's decision to rely solely on the precision of the template, when instead, the investigative report said, the space agency should have been alert "to the fragility of the process and the possibility of error." Managers at NASA apparently paid little attention to the details of the telescope's construction. "There were at least three cases where there was clear evidence that a problem had developed, and it was missed all three times," said Lew Allen, the director of NASA's Jet Propulsion Laboratory and the head of the Hubble investigating committee.

If the Hubble blunder weren't mortifying enough for NASA, just days after announcing the telescope's failure, the agency was forced to ground the entire space-shuttle fleet indefinitely because of hydrogen leaks in the fuel lines, a problem that might have caused another *Challenger*-type tragedy. With the space shuttle out of action, there was no way to ferry up replacement parts to fix Hubble. "I find myself saying to myself, 'Oh no, not again. What's gone wrong?'" said Kent Hughes of the Council on Competitiveness. "Hubble is a little humbling."

Indeed, the whole embarrassing episode seemed to buttress the notion that the United States is a sunset power, incapable of repeating the technological exploits of the past. Daisaku Harada, head of the U.S. office of the Japan Productivity Center, predicted that Hubble's problems would have "a very negative impact" on Japan's perceptions of U.S. competence. Not that the Japanese were all that impressed to begin with. Many Japanese still remember that an American corporation, Boeing, was responsible for the August 1985 crash of a Japan Air Lines 747 northwest of Tokyo, a catastrophe that claimed the lives of 520 people. An investigation revealed that Boeing had incorrectly repaired a bulkhead, which blew off and wrecked the jet's tail section. Not surprisingly, U.S. automobiles sell poorly in Japan partly because the Japanese believe, not without reason, that they are defective and unreliable. How good can they be, the Japanese wonder, when the engineering that goes into such showcase American products as the space shuttle seems so slipshod? At least one Japanese official has vowed that the space shuttle Japan plans to build will not shed tiles from its body during re-entry, as American versions do.

The Japanese are hardly alone in their disillusionment. Many Americans are disappointed by the recent parade of costly bungles by an agency that once seemed to epitomize American competence and technological proficiency. The thrill is gone for many of us; we no longer take space exploration seriously. Having lost faith, we are inclined to believe what scientists told us all along: space is just that, full of nothing.

Some of this is inevitable, of course. The space shuttle lacks the glamour and magic of those audacious *Apollo* moon flights, when we were testing our limits, daring the unknown, "pushing the outside of the envelope." To many, the space shuttles are little more than cosmic trucks, the U-Hauls of the universe. They are the space vehicles of a service-industry America, opening no new territory, staking out no new frontiers, simply running the same old routes and making the same old orbital bus stops.

President Bush has tried to stir up some of that old-time religion with his talk of landing a man on Mars. But somehow that seems too chimerical, too impractical. Many Americans question how sincerely Bush will pursue his extraterrestrial aims (after all, he deputized Chief Space Cadet Danny Quayle to lead the charge), and they wonder where the money (an estimated $80 billion) will come from, and whether, when you get right down to it, America still has the moxie and know-how and derring-do — the right stuff — to rocket human beings to a planet thirty-five million miles away and bring them back alive. They may have a point. After all, would *you* want to travel in a spaceship that far, and that long (two and a half years, round trip), knowing it was made in the U.S.A. — the same country that gave the world the Pinto and the Gremlin?

Maybe none of this bothers you. Maybe you're pleased by the demise of the space program. Maybe you're among those who believe it's a colossal waste, nothing more than an anachronistic display of national machismo. Reaching for the moon and stars was a form of chauvinistic chest-beating by an exuberant country still reveling in its teenage muscularity, still exulting in its boundless powers and seeming invincibility, still trying to dazzle the rest of the world with breathtaking celestial acrobatics. By now, we should be more mature and mellow and not so consumed with proving ourselves. We should be devoting our energies and limited resources to more important, pressing problems here on Earth, in our own country, in our own back yards, problems such as our dilapidated cities, drug-infested neighborhoods, the AIDS epidemic, housing, education, mass transportation, the decaying infrastructure of bridges, roads, and water and sewer systems, and on and on and on.

But to adopt such a view is to discount something essential about the American spirit. This nation was founded and built by people who were unhappy, people who were trying to escape oppression and persecution, poverty and ignorance, people who wanted something more, something better. That has always been the engine of our national progress — the desire for something more, something better. It is this desire that's at the heart of the American Dream. It was this desire that drove us through the War of Independence, that drove us through the Cumberland Gap, that drove us to annex new territories, to battle the elements and tame the wilderness, to push on and on, farther and farther west, in search of the Promised Land, to California and the Pacific, Hawaii and Alaska, and then, when we ran out of land, into outer space, and then to the moon, all in quest of something more, something better.

What does it mean that we've lost our desire to explore and conquer outer space? What happens to us when we no longer honor such an obvious symbol of our national dream? Is it just coincidence that after we reached the moon, back in 1969, we began a period of fierce self-absorption, when for many Americans the only universe worth exploring was the interior world of their own "needs" and whims? Wasn't it significant that the Age of Apollo was followed by the Age of Aquarius, an era of daffy mysticism and moronic psychobabble during which many Americans "actualized" themselves by looking out for number one, jogging, Rolfing, est-ing, swinging, swapping, marinating in hot tubs, stalking sensation, and prostrating before the latest self-help guru and cult prophet?

Viewing American society anthropomorphically, I'd say we are making a rather rough passage through middle age, that we are wrestling with a major midlife crisis. We've gained enough wisdom and insight to realize that we are not perfect and that we have serious problems that could threaten our health and survival. To our credit, we've become expert at identifying what ails us, and analyzing our shortcomings, and flagellating ourselves — at times to an almost pathological degree — for not living up to our potential. But we've also lost so much of our youthful pep and bravery that it's questionable whether, in the end, we have the will and the vigor — the competence — to confront our problems and retain our national greatness.

How have things come to such a sorry pass? Why are we drowning in a sea of incompetence? Many factors are responsible, but as I see it there are five that are paramount: the decline of morals, the decline of the family, the decline of education, the decline of the work ethic, and the decline of quality. They are interrelated, and they reflect and reinforce one another. Nevertheless, one can posit a rough chain of cause and effect. The decline of morals has led to the decline of the family; the decline of the family has led to the decline of education; the decline of education has led to the decline of the work ethic; and the decline of the work ethic has led to the decline of quality.

When the family is no longer sacrosanct, when education is abysmal, when people are lazy and careless in their work, when the goods and services those people provide are of inferior quality, the nation's morals — our mores, our customs, our sense of good and bad, what's right and wrong, the proper way to live — slip another notch. The circle completes and perpetuates itself, America rides yet another loop down the spiral, and incompetence becomes even more pervasive and ingrained.

Lately, there has developed such a body of declinist literature that one naturally grows skeptical, wondering whether this is just another intellectual fad, a manifestation of the regular swing from optimism to pessimism, from euphoria to despair, the consequences of which are ultimately meaningless in light of the United States' history of preternatural resiliency.

I wish I could be comforted by such a thought. I wish I could be more sanguine. But whenever I'm tempted to adopt a rosier perspective, I consider the five factors, and immediately all doubt vanishes about the direction in which America's heading. We have gone from Neil Armstrong to Michael Jackson, from reaching for the stars to being a "star," from George Washington and Thomas Jefferson and James Madison and the profound philosophical meditations about proper government and the rights of man embodied in *The Federalist Papers* to the prepackaged, ghost-written, lip-synced sound bites of Ronald Reagan and George Bush.

Such is what passes for progress today in the United States of Incompetence.

3 The Decline of Morals

A 49-year-old father:

"Sometimes I think the only moral principle in effect these days is 'anything goes.' It's the rationale of 'wilding' youths and take-under-the-table corporate execs. It's the reason there's no such thing as foul language anymore. And there's no such thing as obscenity anymore. And almost any act of violence or sexual perversion will sooner or later show up in the movies or on TV . . .

"Our morals have eroded because we no longer believe in the idea that we survive through our children, that we're living for something larger — to protect freedom, to build the nation, to make a better world for our descendants. That whole idea of a larger purpose has been destroyed in our time. Even agnostics used to say: Whether or not there's a god, we ought to live as if there is. That notion has perished. People today are adrift and don't know what they want. They think the next purchase, the next job, the next degree, the next house, the next lover, the next marriage is suddenly going to make life complete. But of course that never happens. That's not the way it works . . .

"Yesterday's hippies have become today's yuppies. The name of the game now is greed: to acquire as much as you possibly can, as quickly as you can, with the least amount of effort and expense. Everybody's a little Donald Trump; the pleasure is mainly in the acquiring, not in the using and enjoying . . . It reached a climax in the eighties, when

getting and spending was glamorized and glorified. There
was no thought of doing good, or creating value, or making a
contribution, or leaving something behind. It was all,
What's in it for me? I just wanna have fun . . .

"They say that when an organism starts to die, all the
systems that kept it alive start to work to kill it. I think
that's what's happening in America, and I'm deeply worried
about the kind of society our children and grandchildren
will have to inherit."

N o society can function without widely accepted norms
of behavior and standards of conduct. Since the 1960s,
those norms and standards have been battered in the United
States. In the name of freedom and fulfillment, we Americans
have become self-centered, irresponsible, and undisciplined.
We lack self-control and a sense of stewardship. Knowingly,
we are squandering our resources and shortchanging our children. Our promises are enforced by lawyers. The wheels of
commerce and industry are greased by sleaze. Our iniquitous
culture excretes such covetous grotesques as Donald Trump
and Leona Helmsley, such insolent hypocrites as James Watt
and Jim Bakker. In the face of growing social problems, we an-
esthetize ourselves with drugs and mindless TV, shirking responsibility, grabbing for all the gusto we can get, boogieing
into the apocalypse.

Many of us no longer believe in anything above and beyond ourselves. We have lost faith in the afterlife — not only
the religious afterlife but also the future and the idea of a better tomorrow. We don't care about building something for
generations yet to come. We don't care about posterity. We
don't care, in some cases, about our own children and grandchildren. The only thing that matters is this moment and our
personal pleasure. Ours is a society where public school drop-

outs prostitute their bodies for a quick hit of crack, and Ivy League graduates prostitute their minds for a quick killing on Wall Street.

There are those who lament that we've lost our gentility, that we've lost our manners and politeness. Actually, we've gone far, far beyond that today. We have lost our civility — that mutual respect among citizens which is the basis for civilization. We have lost what F. Scott Fitzgerald once called "a sense of the fundamental decencies." We've lost our reverence for human life itself.

We pity those savage Third World countries where life is cheap, and we pride ourselves on being an advanced, civilized society. But how civilized are we when children in New York City have begun wearing bulletproof clothing for protection on their way to and from school? How civilized are we when, in the nation's largest city, there were a record twenty-two hundred killings — an average of more than six a day — in 1990? How civilized are we when our nation's capital has the highest homicide rate of any city in America? How civilized are we when the United States has the highest homicide rate — by far — in the industrialized world?

How far is far? Nearly twenty times that of most other nations. According to a recent international survey, among males ages fifteen to twenty-four, the U.S. homicide rate is 21.9 per 100,000. Compare that to 1.4 per 100,000 in France, or 1.2 per 100,000 in England, or 0.5 per 100,000 in Japan. About 23,000 Americans are shot, stabbed, or beaten to death every year, and the number of murders is expected to climb sharply in the decade ahead. Decrying this "growing bloodbath," Senator Joseph R. Biden, Jr., of Delaware, chairman of the Senate Judiciary Committee, recently said, "At the current pace, about 240,000 Americans will be murdered this decade . . . The scale of this plague is hard to imagine. A quarter of a million murders — that is roughly the population of Richmond or Rochester, St. Paul or Des Moines. This devastation would be like every man, woman, and child in one of those cities dying off this decade."

The statistics are appalling enough, but the outrageous carnage is even more repugnant when one becomes acquainted with the victims and the circumstances under which they lost their lives. They include:

▶ A thirty-eight-year-old man, walking home with his sister on New Year's Eve, attacked by a half-dozen youths after he fails to show "respect." He is punched, kicked, beaten with the headboard of a bed and an old bicycle while struggling across lawns and an alley for about three blocks. He is then skewered with a seventeen-inch knife concealed in a walking stick. The two accused murderers are sixteen and fourteen.

▶ A thirty-one-year-old waitress, mangled by a subway train after being shoved by a thief while she tried to wrest away her purse containing some credit cards and one dollar.

▶ A twenty-two-year-old Utah man, visiting New York City to watch the U.S. Open tennis tournament, stabbed to death when he tries to defend his parents from knife-wielding robbers on a subway platform. The robbers are arrested later the same night at a dance club.

▶ A twenty-one-year-old man, father of two, shot in the head after he refuses to hand over his leather jacket. He is one of scores of youths murdered across the nation by robbers demanding expensive jewelry or sneakers.

▶ An eighteen-year-old boy, killed when a sniper with a machine gun fires on his car and riddles it with bullets.

The shots are traced to an apartment-building roof from which young drug-gang members regularly shoot their automatic weapons for thrills.

▶ *A seventeen-year-old boy, accosted by ten thugs while standing on a corner in his neighborhood. He is beaten with baseball bats and shot in the back. One of the attackers hits the victim over the head so hard that his bat breaks.*

▶ *A nine-year-old girl, shot in the head when a bullet fired by a man shooting wildly at an old enemy rips into the car where she's sleeping, waiting to be carried to bed after a day at an amusement park.*

▶ *A three-year-old boy, killed as he sleeps in his family apartment when gunmen fire more than eighteen rounds from semiautomatic pistols through a steel-covered door.*

▶ *A ten-month-old baby, standing in his walker, shot to death by a gunman who fires repeatedly through the door of the boy's grandmother's apartment.*

If murder is the ultimate antisocial act, what does it say about our society when so many fellow citizens think nothing of taking a life, for the sake of a boom box, a few bucks in a wallet, or to avenge being cut off in traffic? And if this cardinal index of American morality is so dismal, is it any surprise that violent crimes of all sorts are exploding, that more people are raped, robbed, and assaulted here than anywhere else on the planet, that Americans are more likely to become victims of violent crimes today than at any time in modern history, that a record 1.1 million Americans are in prison, and that the

United States is, in the words of a March 1991 Senate Judiciary Committee report, "the most violent and self-destructive nation on earth"?

What's even worse, though, is the brazen, remorseless attitude with which such brutal crimes are committed. Police officials speak of a new and more dangerous breed of street criminal, totally devoid of conscience. This mutant strain of urban animal, often deranged by drugs, seems capable of the most bestial and despicable acts without the slightest twinge of guilt. "There is no remorse, there is not the first tear, there is no sense that this is wrong," says Isaac Fulwood, the police chief of Washington, D.C. "There's just a total disregard for life."

Remember the Central Park jogger, the investment banker who was attacked by a gang of "wilding" youths, raped and beaten with a rock, a brick, and a twelve-inch pipe to within an inch of death? Here's how one of her attackers explained the motivation for the vicious assault: "It was something to do. It was fun."

The motto of the University of Pennsylvania is *Leges sine moribus vanae sunt* — "Laws without morals are in vain." The truth of that assertion hardly needs proof. We are living in an era when moral sanctions are so weak as to be nonexistent. Parents, families, neighbors, schools, churches, universities — all the individuals and institutions that once enforced our customs and morals have lost their power. We are still a society of laws, but there is no moral force to support the laws. As a result, they are flouted with defiant impunity.

"What's very deep in our society, since the sixties, is this anti-authority attitude," says the sociologist E. Digby Baltzell. "There has been a total breakdown of authority and standards. We tolerate anything. How many people get caught cheating at Penn? Nobody. I ask my students how can you get fired from Penn? Screwing the president's wife on the lawn in front of College Hall, with everybody cheering. Short of that, you can't get thrown out."

In an interview in *U.S. News & World Report*, James Billington, now the Librarian of Congress and formerly the director of the Woodrow Wilson International Center for Scholars and a history professor at Princeton, said, "Universities often unintentionally convey to young people the sense that self-indulgence is not only permissible but even desirable . . . Young people acquire an unreal sense of freedom — all the privileges of adults with none of the responsibilities. No one — least of all deans or chaplains — speaks out prominently for self-discipline."

Indeed, America's growing immorality and lawlessness are apparent not only on the mean streets of our cities, but also on Main Street and Wall Street. During the Roaring Eighties, when greed was glamorized, there were many other killings besides homicides — killings involving millions of dollars. The perpetrators were clever and well educated, bearing degrees from the most prestigious colleges and universities. They wore tailored suits and silk ties and had important jobs and impressive titles. They possessed all the symbols of success — elegant wives, sprawling mansions in well-manicured suburbs, limousines and chauffeurs, and all the toys they desired. "Players" and movers and market makers, they were regarded as stars of the business world, and fawned over and flattered accordingly. But the Dennis Levines and Ivan Boeskys and Michael Milkens, and all the other stock-market manipulators, inside traders, and junk-bond kings, violated the law as deliberately and ruthlessly as any ghetto drug lord. In their gluttonous pursuit of bigger deals and bigger bucks, they followed only one principle: their own self-aggrandizement.

Thankfully, the 1980s are over, but the wreckage wrought by the predators of Wall Street remains: once-healthy corporations staggering under mountains of debt;

thousands of long-time employees thrown out of work because of the venal machinations of buccaneer capitalists. There are other bills to pay, too, like the $500 billion it may eventually cost to bail out all the thrift institutions and savings and loans that were looted by white-collar crooks so that they could treat themselves to multimillion-dollar estates, yachts, Rolls-Royces, gold-plated toilets, and museum-quality art collections — all at your expense and mine. It's estimated that it will cost every American man, woman, and child at least $2000 to pay for the decade-long orgy of plutocratic excess to which very few of us were invited. "It was not thugs in ski masks who drained billions and billions of dollars from the nation's S&Ls," noted *Time.* "It was hundreds of (mostly) respected citizens in pinstripes who, seeing that deregulation had left the door to the vault wide open, walked in and grabbed what they could — or at the very least allowed others to do so."

Strip away the clothes and polish, and many of today's white-collar outlaws are just as amoral and unrepentant as "wilding" ghetto kids. Their business ethic is the legal principle "innocent until proven guilty." Do whatever it takes to boost profits and make millions and protect your plunder, because, no matter how damnable your behavior, you've done nothing wrong until you're caught and convicted. And then, of course, it's not really your fault. It's the fault of "the system," it's the fault of society, it's the fault of the economy, it's the fault of overzealous prosecutors, it's the fault of loosely written laws and poorly policed regulations that made wrongdoing too tempting to resist.

After the collapse of Drexel Burnham Lambert, the Wall Street investment firm that spearheaded the junk-bond craze and unleashed Michael Milken, several employees were interviewed in newspapers and on television. They were angry and upset. But they were not angry at Michael Milken or upset with themselves. They were angry at the government for persecuting their hero and they were upset because they'd been deprived of the opportunity to make more deals and skim off more millions. Not a single one admitted that Drexel Burnham had broken the law and acted dishonorably. Not a single one exhibited any contrition. Similarly, several of the scoundrels fingered in the savings and loan debacle have rationalized their malefactions by insisting that all they did was exploit, perhaps injudiciously, legitimate business opportunities made more attractive by the government's willingness to back up their gambles. So, really, they argue, no one person's to blame; everybody's to blame.

"If it's everybody's fault, it is no one's in particular," wrote the columnist George F. Will. "From that conclusion, it is a short slither to blaming the 'system,' and from there it is but a hop, skip and a jump into sociology: the *Zeitgeist* did it! You know: the 1980s, glitz, BMWs and Rolex watches, bury my heart in the Hamptons — yuppies. In a word, the culprit was greed, which may technically be traceable to Adam's fall but really got ripping only after Reagan's inauguration. There is nothing like a fine mist of sociology for obscuring responsibility."

Free will is the glory of human nature; it is the capacity to choose — right or wrong, good or bad — that makes us moral creatures. Free will implies responsibility, for the choices each of us makes we make alone and those choices define our character. Today, it seems, more and more people are abdicating that responsibility and hence, implicitly, their own free will. One commentator calls it "the blame game," and it's the reason that, at all levels of society, individual accountability has virtually disappeared.

At the top, politicians and corporate chieftains rarely acknowledge their mistakes or pay for their blunders. Standard practice these days is to accept responsibility — but none of the blame. If a Japanese corporation had caused a catastrophe like the *Exxon Valdez* spill, the CEO undoubtedly would have resigned, for the Japanese still have a strong sense of personal responsibility and shame. But we Americans are an enlightened nation, a nation that has transcended such primitive notions as sin and guilt, a nation where all wrongdoing is the fault of bad genes or a wretched environment or a psychological disease, a nation where errors and failures and criminal charges are merely embarrassing PR problems to be "managed" by "stonewalling" and "toughing it out."

When Marion Barry, the mayor of Washington, D.C., was arrested for smoking crack cocaine, he employed a strategy that's becoming popular today: he portrayed himself as the victim of a racist government conspiracy, and at one point even accused federal prosecutors of trying to kill him by letting him smoke the crack during the videotaped sting operation. His rationale was quickly embraced by other black leaders. Benjamin Hooks, executive director of the NAACP, announced to three thousand convention delegates that Barry's prosecution was part of the government's "incessant harassment of black elected officials." Suddenly, Marion Barry was not a drug user who had demeaned his office, betrayed his constituents, and embarrassed his city; he was a hero. He was applauded by black politicians and clergy. At a meeting of black mayors, he received a standing ovation. He was transformed into a cultural symbol and racial martyr, thus legitimating the practice of ducking responsibility and blaming personal failures on such abstract scapegoats as racism, drugs, poverty, etc.

The fact is, as federal prosecutors argued in a brief filed in the case, "no one forced [Barry] to go to the hotel room at the Vista Hotel; no one forced him to ask for drugs; no one forced him to buy crack; no one forced him to put a portion of the crack in his jacket pocket to take with him; and no one forced him to smoke the crack. To the contrary, he deliberately engaged in this criminal conduct as he had on scores of other similar occasions."

Barry, of course, isn't the only black American to invoke the "R word" to excuse his misdeeds. Rabble-rousing charlatans like Louis Farrakhan and Al Sharpton peddle a gospel of victimhood whose essential theme is that all the pathologies of the black community are the fault of the white power structure and white racists. Some blacks believe in what's called "the Conspiracy" or "the Plan." In its most extreme version, "the Plan" is nothing less than a plot to exterminate blacks, a plot devised by white leaders and directed from the subbasement of the White House.

Such hallucinations may be exculpatory, but they won't help the so-called underclass rescue itself from misery and impoverishment. "It's not the Klan or skinheads making the black community a hostile economic climate, causing its people to live in daily fear of loss of life and property, or preventing academic excellence," Walter E. Williams, a professor of economics at George Mason University pointed out, in a column published in the *Philadelphia Inquirer*. "If we pretend that racism is the culprit, we then concede that we black people have no control over our destiny and any improvement must await the moral rejuvenation of white people.

"Holding black people accountable for shortcomings frequently encounters the pseudo-intellectual charge of 'blaming the victim,' which is a moral retreat and a mindless copout. It says that while we may criticize others for self-destructive behavior, black people are to be exempt. Such a position denies human responsibility."

Julius Lester, the 1960s black radical who wrote *Look Out, Whitey! Black Power's Gon' Get Your Mama*, is now a professor of Jewish studies at the University of Massachusetts. In a recent speech before the National Forum Foundation, he said, "The shift from fighting for civil rights to fighting against racism was a shift from seeking and finding common ground to a position that has been disastrously divisive. To fight against racism divides humanity into 'us against them.' It leads to a self-definition as 'victim' and anyone who defines himself as a victim has found a way to keep himself in a perpetual state of self-righteous self-pity and anger. And that, in a nutshell, is the state of black America today."

Actually, it's the state of America today, period. "There's a tremendous cult of the victim, a tremendous feeling sorry for people who are just plain irresponsible and sexually promiscuous," says Baltzell. "It's all a lack of moral control."

As AIDS continues to kill some of the nation's most creative and talented people, gay activists have become more militant, staging disruptive demonstrations to press their demand that the government spend more money — as much as it takes — to halt the plague *right now!* Their insistence at times verges on petulance, tinged with the suggestion that scientists are deliberately dragging their feet or withholding a cure. They portray themselves as victims, not only of a disease but also of an unresponsive, homophobic society. In fact, except for cancer, AIDS now receives more government research money than any other illness in America — about $1.2 billion. That is not enough, homosexuals claim; the government is obligated to do more, until the scourge is stopped.

Yet in all their angry street theater, rarely, if ever, have the gay protesters acknowledged the possibility of personal responsibility. One has great sympathy for those who became infected by AIDS before anything was known about the disease. But today we know that AIDS is contracted in nearly nine out of ten adult cases in one of two ways: by engaging in homosexual sex without a condom or by shooting up drugs with a contaminated needle. In other words, AIDS, for the most part, is the direct consequence of reckless, promiscuous behavior.

Such blunt talk is not welcome today; it marks one, God forbid, as "insensitive" and "judgmental." It smacks of Bible-quoting, right-wing kooks, and is anathema to the culture of victimhood, which is based on a simple principle: the individual is essentially passive and always blameless; therefore anything bad that happens is the fault of malevolent institutions and hostile, uncontrollable social forces.

Not long ago, I received a press release from an organization that is working to halt the surge of teenage pregnancy and illegitimate babies by encouraging schools to begin a program of "education for parenting." That's a laudable idea, and I was sympathetic to the group's mission until I came across this classic example of victimspeak: "Our society does not value or institutionalize the sensitive (nonjudgmental) teaching of values awareness. This deficiency becomes the demographics of alienation and destructive behavior."

You'll notice that the authors of this manifesto regard *sensitive* and *nonjudgmental* as apparently interchangeable synonyms. I'm not sure what "values awareness" actually means, but I do know that the "nonjudgmental teaching of values" is an impossible contradiction. The very word *value* implies a hierarchy of worth, which in turn implies the making of judgments. If, in order to be "sensitive," no "value" is judged to be superior to any other (and therefore all values are equal), then you have no values at all. Furthermore, in keeping with the ideology of victimhood, there is no mention of individual behavior, effort, and responsibility. Instead, human will and self-determination are submerged in benign sociological fog, and the finger is pointed at the usual culprits: society and its laggard institutions are mainly to blame for "the demographics of alienation and destructive behavior" (whatever that means).

Today, the culture of victimhood is not limited to America's racial and sexual minorities. The unwillingness to assume responsibility for one's own actions has spread from the disgruntled fringes and infects the moral outlook of many mainstream Americans. Its most telling manifestation is our latest national entitlement: freedom from risk.

People feel they have a constitutional right to be immune from danger, accidents, bad breaks, and bad luck. If fate does not cooperate, then of course it's someone else's fault. They are encouraged in this juvenile fantasy by a hungry mob of personal-injury and liability lawyers who are all too ready to champion the most preposterous claims in the hope of reaping a windfall by convincing gullible jurors to stick it to deep-pocket corporations and insurance companies.

I read recently about a woman who had the gall to sue a resort hotel in Hawaii because she got knocked down by a wave while walking along the shore. Her gripe? That the hotel "recklessly, carelessly, and with due lack of circumspection allowed a dangerous condition to exist on its beach." What's most frightening is that a real lawyer, presumably a reasonably intelligent person, actually took up this woman's cause.

Then there's the woman who sued the state of New York for $1 million because she got hit by a Frisbee while sunbathing in a public park on Long Island. And the parents of the Little Leaguer who sued an athletic-equipment manufacturer because their son twisted his ankle while sliding into second base. And the patient who sued the estate of his dentist for "abandonment" because the dentist, while performing dental implant surgery on the patient, had the nerve to have a heart attack and die.

In an essay in *The New Republic* entitled "Fear of Living," the late Henry Fairlie observed: "The idea that our individual lives and the nation's life can and should be risk-free has grown to be an obsession, driven far and deep into American attitudes. Indeed, the desire for a risk-free society is one of the most debilitating influences in America today, progressively enfeebling the economy with a mass of safety regulations and a widespread fear of liability rulings, and threatening to create an unbuoyant and uninventive society ... This morbid aversion to risk calls into question how Americans now envision the destiny of their country."

This loss of courage, faith, and individual responsibility is reflected most ominously in the growth of one of America's biggest boom industries: tort law. Tort law threatens to make the economy uncompetitive and warps the American legal system and its judicial philosophy. As Peter W. Huber wrote in *Liability: The Legal Revolution and Its Consequences*, "No other country in the world administers anything like it." Tort law was "set in place in the 1960s and 1970s by a new generation of lawyers and judges . . . Some grew famous and more grew rich in selling their services to enforce the rights they themselves invented."

Our readiness to sue others for our own stupidity and misfortune is, with the support of lawyers, judges, and juries, producing a "tort tax" on goods and services that amounts to a $300 billion levy on the American economy. The tort tax, according to Huber, accounts for 30 percent of the price of a stepladder and 95 percent of the price of childhood vaccines. Meanwhile, the award of huge and often unjustifiable punitive damages is frustrating, if not crushing, the spirit of innovation in American business.

"There used to be eighteen companies making football helmets in this country, but the liability crisis has pared them down to just two," noted Lee Iacocca, chairman of Chrysler, in a recent speech. "Nobody makes gymnastics or hockey equipment anymore. Too risky. A small company in Virginia that made driving aids for handicapped people went out of business because it couldn't afford the liability insurance. Too risky. We've virtually stopped making light aircraft in this country; the biggest production cost is the liability insurance. Too risky. One of these days, we're going to wake up and say, 'The hell with it — competing is just too risky!' Why even try to build a better mousetrap? Let somebody else do it — and then sue him."

A 1988 Conference Board survey of CEOs showed that concern over potential liability had led almost 50 percent of the companies to discontinue product lines, and nearly 40 percent to withhold new products, including beneficial drugs. Richard Neely, a justice of the West Virginia Supreme Court and the author of *The Product Liability Mess,* complains that much of his time on the bench is "devoted to ways to make business pay for everyone else's bad luck."

And *luck* is the operative word. At a time when the belief in an afterlife is declining, people are obsessed with instant gratification, getting theirs here and now, striking it rich, hitting it big, getting something for nothing. Consider the experience of SEPTA, the regional transit authority that runs the buses, trolleys, subways, and commuter trains in and around Philadelphia. In fiscal 1990, SEPTA was barraged with more than 10,300 legal claims, and paid out an estimated $47 million in settlements. That's 17.7 percent of the amount it collected in fares, a higher percentage than any other transit authority in the United States. "There is no place in the country with the tort law we have, or the number of personal-injury lawyers," says the SEPTA general counsel James F. Kilcur, who calls Philadelphia "the claims capital of the nation."

Many of the claims are fraudulent — flat-out, bald-faced, trumped-up lies. A few years ago, a SEPTA bus hit a telephone pole. "People ran out of their homes to try to get on the bus," recalls Robert Wert, a former SEPTA counsel. "It's not a joke; it's a tragedy." In June 1988, after a car collided with a bus, eleven people filed suit against SEPTA, demanding compensation for various injuries. Trouble is, the bus was empty.

Such blatant attempts to milk "the system" should come as no surprise in an age when far too many Americans have an "attitude" — namely, that life is just another lottery, a one-time spin of the roulette wheel, so you're a fool if you don't try to better your odds, exploit every advantage, and wangle all you can out of every roll of the dice.

"To a few 'unalienable rights' have been added an endless array of wishes and whims, all taking root as rights, all legitimized by those eager to swing the courthouse doors open wide to consider every imaginable gripe, complaint, and grievance," wrote the lawyer Gerald K. McOscar in the *Philadelphia Inquirer*. "The legal system more and more resembles a gigantic game of Trivial Pursuit ... which pits neighbor against neighbor and group against group."

In a nation with such an ethos, is it any wonder that products are shoddy, service is surly, and the phony and greedy are exalted? Is it any wonder that incompetence is ubiquitous and our lives are dominated by the tawdry and schlocky?

It wasn't always this way.

There was a time when America's manners and morals were better. There was a time when most Americans lived in the same small town or city neighborhood their entire lives. They grew up among sisters and brothers, uncles and aunts, cousins and grandparents, neighbors and friends, teachers and ministers who knew who they were. In the process, they developed a strong sense of family and community, a sense of where they fit in, a sense of right and wrong, a sense of what was acceptable and what was not. The norms of the community were upheld by everyday contact with people whose approval or disapproval counted. Sure, there was wrongdoing and hypocrisy and evil, but those tempted to misbehave or defy convention were usually inhibited by a clearly defined set of social sanctions.

For some, that way of life was comforting and nurturing, the very essence of "home"; for others, it was stifling and maddening, a goad to bust out of town for the bright lights of the big city. That way of life had undeniable advantages and drawbacks, but it is useless to discuss them now. Times change, and that way of life has almost vanished. Today, because ours is such a mobile, transient society, most of us are not living where we grew up. In search of adventure and excitement and high-paying, high-prestige jobs, many of us have settled in or near big cities, leaving the folks and home-town buddies back in Texas or Missouri or West Virginia.

As a result, we are dwelling, by and large, among strangers, in apartments and suburban subdivisions where, even after years, we may not know the name of the person next door. In some urban neighborhoods, the hoods and thugs are so dominant that law-abiding citizens have become prisoners in their own homes, afraid to venture out for fear they'll be cut down in the crossfire of automatic weapons. In the suburbs, people distance themselves from others and a menacing world by erecting stockade fences and surrounding their split-level sanctuaries with a verdant moat of Kentucky bluegrass.

Once upon a time, America was a gregarious, other-directed front-porch society. Then, in the fifties or thereabouts, we became a more private back yard society. Today, it seems, we are a family-room society, huddled in the darkness, watching the flickering shadows on the TV screen, which connects us electronically to the global village, where people are nothing more than evanescent images, and our best friend is likely to be Phil Donahue or Alex Trebek, and *community* is the good folks and fun in a McDonald's commercial.

We still salute the *idea* of community, of course; it is, after all, so much a part of the American myth — *e pluribus unum*, and all that. But meanwhile, in the real America, midnight screams for help are ignored because no one wants to get involved; volunteer fire companies are closing because no one wants to join; Memorial Day parades and other binding rituals are a thing of the past because no one wants to be bothered; telephone books are thinner because more and more people want their numbers unlisted.

For some, the lack of community is positive and desirable. It affords anonymity, which can be liberating and exhilarating. It means freedom from the obligations of neighborliness, and the judgments and censure of prying gossips and narrow-minded busybodies. It is the reason cities, where the rootless congregate and the sense of community is generally weakest, are magnets for nonconformists and mavericks.

In general, though, the breakdown of community is unhealthy. It means alienation, disconnectedness, anomie, the absence of moral standards, and the loss of moral authority. Without community, there is ignorance and suspicion. Ignorance and suspicion lead to distrust, and distrust is the petri dish for prejudice and bigotry. As our community spirit flags, it is hardly surprising that the United States is splintering into tribes of warring pseudocommunities. Instead of a melting pot, we've become a boiling, bitter stew of racial, ethnic, and sexual minorities — united by grudge, pursuing special interests, making "non-negotiable" demands — and all too eager to believe the worst of each other.

Perhaps we've reached the point where genuine community is no longer possible in the United States. Perhaps our society is too large and too diverse to support a national consensus about values and morals. It's significant to me that so many fundamental moral issues — chief among them abortion — are being dealt with in courts of law, and decided by such slim majorities of judges and voters that the principle seems to stand only until the next election. It is significant too that so many Americans feel compelled today to identify themselves as Irish-Americans or Polish-Americans or African-Americans — and that it's what parts us rather than what joins us that so consumes us today.

On a recent vacation trip, my wife and I were stranded in Roanoke, Virginia, on a day of incessant, torrential rain, with a cranky five-year-old in tow. Desperate, we spotted a shopping mall on the outskirts of town with a movie theater showing *Batman*. Our son, Teddy, having absorbed plenty of

Batman ballyhoo on TV, was eager to see it. The movie was rated PG, but the usher assured us the movie would be just fine for a five-year-old. So we bought our tickets.

I was expecting *Batman* to be harmless, corny, and camp, a gaudy comic book adventure like the *Superman* movies. Two hours later, I left the theater feeling ashamed, angry, and depressed. I was ashamed because I'd exposed my son to a movie that was dark and sinister, a movie that glorified violence and sadism in a creepy atmosphere of carefree anarchy. I was angry at those who made the movie for being callous, cynical, and irresponsible. And I was depressed because of what the movie said about American morals. This movie, after all, ignited no public furor, was positively tame by "slasher" standards, and was hailed by most critics as fun, inspired, and faithful to the spirit of the original characters. But as I recalled the vicious, lurid fight scenes, the Joker disfiguring a woman's face with acid, and his goons defacing paintings and breaking statues in a museum (accompanied by a driving, libidinous, upbeat score by Prince), I was filled with dread for the kind of nation my son and millions of other children will someday inherit and have to live in.

In our atomized, secular society, at a time when political and religious figures are unable to command respect, to inspire, and to lead, the mass media — television, movies, radio, records, advertising, magazines, newspapers, and books — have emerged as the only agencies capable of reaching us all, of shaping a national consciousness, of bringing us as close to community as we're likely to get. Collectively, the media have unprecedented power to disseminate new ideas, images, and products. They are supplanting the family, school, and church in establishing norms and articulating mores. Merely by selecting and amplifying, they celebrate and implicitly endorse. Their influence is enormous, and so is their responsibility.

But too often the media shirk that responsibility and

abuse their power. Since they are constantly vying for our attention, they are compelled to seek out, exploit, and hype the latest, the glitziest, the most sensational. The result? Blood and gore — packaged in such brutal flicks as *Die Hard II*, *Robocop*, *Terminator*, and *Total Recall* — are generously splattered on every multiplex movie screen from Bangor to Buena Vista. And the "F word" has become so common that the industry's conservative ratings board doesn't even bother to punish the occasional use of it with a restrictive R rating. On MTV, the moment's hot rock stars engage in ritualized copulation; on network television, sit-com moms elicit snickers with innuendoes about oral sex. In a week's time, the average viewer sees 150 acts of violence and 15 murders. As for popular music . . .

Well, consider the contributions of the rap group called the Geto Boys. In one of their songs, "Mind of a Lunatic," the narrator slashes a woman's throat and then has sex with the corpse. In another song, the narrator describes a sexual act that culminates when his partner's head explodes from a shotgun blast.

Then, of course, there's 2 Live Crew, whose rap album *As Nasty As They Wanna Be* features more profanity than you'll hear from the foulest-mouthed drill sergeant. The album is only seventy-nine minutes long, but, according to Focus on Family, an evangelical group, the rappers say "fuck" 226 times, "bitch" 163 times, refer to male and female genitalia 117 times, and describe oral sex 87 times. Their message is misogyny, specifically that women are creatures who deserve to be used and abused, and it's delivered in such memorable "lyrics" as "He'll tear the pussy open 'cause it's satisfaction" and "Grabbed one by the hair, threw her on the floor, opened up her thighs and guess what I saw?" In one song, 2 Live Crew extols the thrill of forcing anal sex on a girl and making her lick excrement.

Amazingly — or perhaps predictably — 2 Live Crew has

its defenders. Pleading for more understanding, Henry Louis Gates, a professor of English at Duke University, argues that the rap group is simply "engaged in heavy-handed parody, turning the stereotypes of black and white American culture on their heads. These young artists are acting out, to lively dance music, a parodic exaggeration of the age-old stereotypes of the oversexed black female and male. Their exuberant use of hyperbole (phantasmagoric sexual organs, for example) undermines — for anyone fluent in black cultural codes — a too literal-minded hearing of the lyrics."

What a crock of highfalutin poppycock. The fact remains that it's impossible to imagine "music" that is more explicit, vulgar, cruel, offensive, and repulsive. As John Leo observed in *U.S. News & World Report:* "The issue at the heart of the controversy over the rap group 2 Live Crew is not censorship, artistic freedom, sex, or even obscene language. The real problem, I think, is this: Because of the cultural influence of one not very distinguished rap group, 10- and 12-year-old boys now walk down the street chanting about the joys of damaging a girl's vagina during sex."

Sadly, many of 2 Live Crew's apologists are so hung up on the censorship issue that they're utterly unable to appreciate the awfulness — and the awful consequences — of what they're promoting. "Most people, and in particular 2 Live Crew's intellectual defenders, fervently believe in the connection between good art and the good society," the syndicated columnist Charles Krauthammer wrote recently. "If they did not think that good art is elevating, artists would not make it and the people would not support it. And yet the corollary — if good art can elevate, then bad art can degrade — is a proposition they refuse to grasp . . .

"As a psychiatrist, I used to see patients who, urged on by voices inside their heads, did crazy and terrible things, like immolating themselves. Now we have legions of kids walking around with the technological equivalent: 2 Live Crew wired by Walkman directly into their brains, proposing to 'bust your pussy, then break your backbone . . . I wanna see you bleed.' Surprised that a whole generation is busting and breaking and bleeding? Culture has consequences."

If popular culture reflects our morals, how can anyone deny that our society has now, with the aural filth of rappers like 2 Live Crew, degenerated to a new evolutionary low? It is certainly a long way down from Victor Herbert and Cole Porter and Frank Sinatra and even Elvis and the Four Tops and the Supremes and the Temptations. Remember when songs had melodies and appealed to the heart and lifted the soul? Remember when pop musicians earned acclaim by daring to be sentimental?

Not so today. The *Washington Post* columnist Richard Cohen wrote, "It's as if neither these young men nor their listeners connect at all with romance and love, tenderness and affection. They seem to think that cynicism is an adult characteristic, when, it turns out, it is really a characteristic of youth . . . The same cynicism, the same hardness, can be seen in the movies, especially those favored by young men. The movies of Arnold Schwarzenegger and Sylvester Stallone do for the pain and suffering of war what pornography does for sex. They're unfeeling."

The late Norman Cousins, who was editor of *The Saturday Review* and a faculty member of the School of Medicine at the University of California at Los Angeles, made a similar point in *Time:* "Violence in language has become almost as casual as the possession of handguns. The curious notion has taken hold that emphasis in communicating is impossible without the incessant use of four-letter words. The effect is to foster attitudes of casualness toward violence and brutality not just in entertainment but in everyday life . . . The ability to react instinctively to suffering seems to be atrophying. Youngsters sit transfixed in front of television or motion-picture screens, munching popcorn while human beings are battered or mutilated. Nothing is more essential in education than respect for the frailty of human beings; nothing is more characteristic of the age than mindless violence."

I do not consider myself a prude or a bluenose (nor do those who know me). As a journalist, I hold the First Amendment sacred and believe in freedom of expression and freedom of information. I abhor censorship or thought control in any form, and I'm disturbed when the state tries to dictate and police what people can say, read, and see. But I also believe in exercising our First Amendment freedoms responsibly, carefully, and thoughtfully so that the fruits of those freedoms serve to exalt and ennoble us and make us more humane, tender, and civilized.

Too often that is plainly not the case. Many people in the movie, television, and radio business, many editors of newspapers, magazines, and books, don't seem to care whether what they produce has any redeeming social value as long as it attracts viewers, listeners, and readers. Many people in the media generate information and ideas conscientiously and create art and entertainment that edify and endure. But many others seem to be motivated by nothing more lofty than maximizing the gross — in both senses of the word.

For the past fourteen years, I've worked at a big-city East Coast newspaper with a highly regarded staff dominated by bright, talented baby boomers who came of age during the 1960s. Many of the journalists I know — at the *Inquirer* and elsewhere — pride themselves on being hip, trendy, and on the cutting edge of what's hot and what's happening. Some are transplanted small-towners who, eager to erase any trace of provincialism, affect a swank, with-it urban worldliness or the ethereal hauteur of the terminally artsy and avant-garde. Some are arrogant experts and technocrats, often long on cosmic ideals and short on personal scruples, who believe their intellectual sophistication exempts them from any sort of conventional morality.

Some are former hippies who've never outgrown their counterculture contempt for government, religion, and other Establishment institutions. Many hold degrees from the nation's premier colleges, and they use their educations to stoke a critical intelligence that is forever analyzing, tearing down, and ridiculing — whether it be stories, movies, books, plays, or the politics, style, or character of others. Glib and clever, bred to worship "openness" and "diversity," they subscribe to the tenets of moral relativism and secular humanism, and pride themselves on being "sensitive," "nonjudgmental," and "value neutral" — though they're quick to shun those who deviate from the fashionable groupthink and reigning political orthodoxy. Professionally, they follow the dictum of Finley Peter Dunne: to comfort the afflicted and afflict the comfortable. Smug about their conspicuous compassion, they are sympathetic to the assertion of personal "rights" but reticent about the need for discipline, obligation, self-reliance, and responsibility.

For many, freedom — and particularly freedom of expression — is a fetish, and their highest ambition can be summarized in three words: *épater la bourgeoisie* — shock the ordinary folks who still believe in God, country, and decency. No creative endeavor is worthy, no art is truly art unless it provokes and outrages the culturally benighted middle class and the boorish denizens of suburbia. And so they snicker and snort at the paintings of Andrew and Jamie Wyeth, which they dismiss as too representational, too comprehensible, and thus too pedestrian. But when the heavies from the National Endowment for the Arts threaten to cut off funding for the likes of Robert Mapplethorpe (noted for photographing himself with a bullwhip protruding from his rectum), and Andres Serrano (noted for taking a picture of a crucifix immersed in urine), and Karen Finley (noted for smearing her body with chocolate and putting alfalfa sprouts in her crotch), they unfurl the banner of the First Amendment, with reflexive swiftness, and rush to the barricades to defend Art, never pausing to consider the nature of what they're advocating (would they hang Mapplethorpe's endearing photos of sodomizing couples in their child's room? Would they feel any differently if Serrano had submerged a Jewish star or a picture of the Reverend Martin Luther King, Jr., in piss?) or that such "art" might gravely offend a vast majority of Americans, and that the issue is not, and never was, censorship or suppression but whether all taxpayers, philistine though they may be, should be compelled, through the NEA, to subsidize such fruitcakes and underwrite the creation and presentation of such rubbish.

With such people working the levers of the media — shaping opinion, influencing taste, engineering reality — how can anyone be surprised that our morals are deteriorating and our society is in disarray? And with the media constantly exhorting us to cast off our inhibitions and indulge ourselves now, is it any wonder that so many Americans, having acquired the habit of seeing everything and doing anything, run the risk of feeling nothing?

4 The Decline of the Family

A 66-year-old grandmother:
"There's a lot of chaos in families today. When I was growing up, families were more closely knit. My parents had no education but they did the best they could with the knowledge they had. They were immigrants, they were poor — I mean really poor. We didn't have all the luxuries that the children have today. But they provided us with a nice clean home and good healthy food and they understood what it takes to make a family and raise children: love, attention, structure, and discipline.

"Parents today don't have the same dedication. They get married on a whim and stay married for their own convenience. They don't have the perseverance that we had. They have a disagreement or an argument and they're ready to pack up. They give up entirely too easily, mainly because there's nothing that holds them together but material things.

"I know it's a must for husbands and wives to work today. My heart goes out to young people who are trying to raise children when a pair of sneakers costs $50 and house prices are so outrageous. But I think some parents are too caught up in their own interests and pleasures. They're chasing luxuries they think will make them happy and they've lost sight of what really matters. By the time they get home from work they're so exhausted they have nothing left for their kids.

"In many homes, there's no family life anymore. Parents are so absorbed doing their own thing that they're not spending enough time doing things together with their kids. Everybody's running around in all different directions. There's no traditional get-together at dinner time where you discuss the kind of day you had and talk over problems. Some parents are so tied up with work and activities that half the time they don't know where their kids are or what they're doing. Maybe because they're too tired or maybe because they're feeling guilty, they're far too lax and permissive. There's no structure, there's no discipline, and kids need that as much as they do love . . .

"Many children today are growing up lonely. I worked as a classroom aide at an elementary school for several years and it just broke my heart. A lot of the children were lacking love. Most of them came from broken homes, and half of them didn't know who their parents were. We had blue cards for them designating who to call in case of an emergency. When they got sick, you would call those numbers, and nobody would respond. Neither one of the parents would come. And these poor kids would sit there all day long with their heads on their desks, feeling sick and abandoned."

T HE BENJAMIN FRANKLIN PARKWAY in Philadelphia is modeled after the Champs-Élysées in Paris. It is a broad boulevard flanked by stately stone buildings with massive columns and classical decorations. One of those magnificent buildings houses the Family Court of Philadelphia, and the contrast between the ordered architecture outside — with its explicit allusions to the glories of past civilizations — and what goes on inside could hardly be more striking and disheartening. For Philadelphia's Family Court is a window through which one can see, with frightening clarity, the disintegration of the American family at its most extreme.

In waiting rooms outside the courtrooms sit grandmothers, aunts, and other relatives who've come to seek custody of children whose parents are so strung out on heroin, crack, or other drugs that they are incapable of caring for their sons and daughters. Today, three out of five custody cases involve some kind of drugs, Doris Harper, supervisor of the child-custody unit, told the *Inquirer*'s Donald Drake. "Might be the mother, might be the father. Sometimes we get cases where the whole family is involved in drugs and alcohol." Mothers as young as eleven have come into the custody unit already addicted to crack. "The family is nothing anymore," Harper says. "It doesn't mean a thing. It doesn't even exist in some cases."

In Philadelphia, calls flood the child-abuse hotline at the rate of 250 a week, each reporting another instance of parental mistreatment or neglect. There are so many battered and abandoned children that social-welfare agencies are overwhelmed. Today, more than fifty-four hundred Philadelphia children are wards of the city's foster-care system. More than sixteen hundred of them are under the age of five — a 98 percent increase since 1985. Nationwide, reports of child abuse have soared from 600,000 in 1979 to 2.4 million in 1989; between 1985 and 1988, the number of American children living in foster homes leaped 23 percent.

The family is breaking down not just in gritty inner-city neighborhoods. It is falling apart in places like Grosse Point, Michigan, and Greenwich, Connecticut, and Silver Spring, Maryland, and Beverly Hills, California, and on the Philadelphia Main Line, those preserves of polished, proper gentry who seem to have everything — gilt pedigrees, ivied educations, sprawling mansions, Mercedes-Benz station wagons, blond children attending the right prep schools.

Yes, even in Status Symbol Land, among the materially

fortunate and presumably enlightened, the family is in critical condition. Those who have brains and beauty and breeding are no more immune than anyone else to family turmoil, to cold, hateful marriages that warp their children's lives and boil over occasionally into scenes right out of *Who's Afraid of Virginia Woolf?*, to consuming career ambitions that monopolize their attention and deprive their children of precious time, to personal insecurity and spiritual bankruptcy that drive them to neglect their families and seek solace in drink or drugs or extramarital lovers or the manic pursuit of money and power and things. Samuel H. Preston, a University of Pennsylvania demographer, says, "My kids attend elite schools in an affluent suburb. Most of their girlfriends and boyfriends come from very troubled families. What kind of scar this is going to leave when these people are adults is not very clear, but we are playing with dynamite."

The decline of the family is documented in academic studies galore as well as in daily newspaper stories and the personal experience of nearly every American citizen: junior high mothers, slowing marriage rates, high divorce rates, falling birth rates, fathers who shirk child support, children reared by the television set. In America today, the traditional family — two parents with children — exists in only 26 percent of households, down from 31 percent in 1980 and 40 percent in 1970. In 1990, the number of single parents hit 9.7 million, up 41 percent from a decade ago. Of those single parents, 8.4 million were single mothers, up 35 percent from 1980. Two million children a year are abused, neglected, or both. Between two and a half million and seven million "latchkey children" under fourteen fend for themselves after school; another million children are runaways.

The younger the children, the more likely they are to be poor. At some point each month, 500,000 of the thirteen million American children living in poverty go hungry. Twelve million youngsters have no medical coverage; five million teeter on the edge of homelessness. Because of insufficient prenatal care, a baby born in the shadow of the White House is now more likely to die in the first year of life than a baby born in Costa Rica.

"We are less committed by any indicator to performance of traditional family roles than we were in the fifties and sixties," says Preston. "Twenty-three percent of the kids are born out of wedlock; of those born in wedlock, half will have parents who separate or divorce in the course of the kids' childhood. The combination of high rates of illegitimacy and marital breakup is such that 60 percent of American children will spend at least part of their childhood living with only one parent."

The decline of the family is, without a doubt, the most serious domestic social problem facing the United States. In the long run, it is far more important than most of the problems and crises that grab the headlines in the daily newspaper. As the basic unit of society, the family is responsible for nurturing the young, shaping values, instilling ethics, transmitting culture, developing competence, and producing contributing citizens. "As the family goes, so goes the nation" is the way it's commonly put. If the saying is true (and there's every reason to believe it is), the United States faces a difficult future — a future of precipitous decline.

"During the past twenty-five years, family decline in the United States has been steeper and more alarming than during any other quarter century in our history," says David Popenoe, a professor of sociology at Rutgers University. "Individual family members have become more autonomous and less bound by the family group, and the group has become less cohesive. The family has lost power and authority to other institutions, especially to the state and its agencies. The family has grown smaller, less stable, and has a shorter life span; people are therefore family members for a smaller percentage of their life.

"The outcome of these trends is that people have become less willing to invest time, money, and energy in family life. It is the individual, not the family unit, in whom the main investments are increasingly being made."

In the United States, more than a million teenagers a year get pregnant, and half of them, usually the poorest, have babies. Across the country, about ten thousand babies a year are born to children under the age of fifteen. This nation has the highest rate of teenage pregnancy among all developed countries; of every six babies born in the United States, one will be the child of a teenage mother; from a fifth to a quarter of all teenage mothers will become pregnant with their second child within a year of having their first; less than 50 percent of teenage mothers graduate from high school; teen fathers are 40 percent less likely to graduate than their peers who are not parents.

In other words, more children — largely uneducated and ignorant children — are having children. And those children are less likely to become competent workers, citizens, and parents; hence, incompetence ramifies and multiplies.

"With rare exceptions, two-parent families are good for children, one-parent families are bad, zero-parent families are horrible," said Chester H. Finn, Jr., a professor of education and public policy at Vanderbilt University, in a recent speech. "This is not something to be ashamed of. It is the product of the species' experience in billions of instances spanning the millennia . . . We know that a well-functioning society must condemn behavior that results in people having children who are not prepared to be good parents. I find it astonishing that, in the face of that knowledge, today we seem to attach more opprobrium to dropping out of school, experimenting on a cat, or uttering nasty remarks on campus than we do to giving birth to what, not so many years ago, were called 'illegitimate' children."

Today, 35 percent of children in the United States live

with one biological parent, and more children are being raised by relatives or in foster homes. Of children born between 1950 and 1954, only 19 percent of whites, and 48 percent of blacks, had lived in a single-parent family by the time they reached seventeen. For white children born in 1980, the figure is projected to soar to 70 percent, and for blacks, to 94 percent.

"The quality of the parent-child bond is deteriorating. Children are spending less and less time with their parents, and particularly less time with their fathers and men in general," says David Blankenhorn, president of the Institute for American Values, a Washington research and public education organization concerned with family issues. In 1960, 11 percent of children were functioning without fathers; in other words, these were kids who never knew their fathers or had not seen their fathers in the past year. Today, that proportion has more than doubled — a situation, says Blankenhorn, that's particularly rough on boys.

Because of the decline of the family, more children are emotionally disturbed and psychologically distressed. "There are very significant differences in the psychological well-being of children from families with a marital disruption," says Preston. "Optimists may say, well, these were families that were in trouble anyway and it might have been worse for the children if the couple had stayed together. But if you ask the children, they don't agree with that. In general, children want their parents to stay together, no matter how much fighting is going on."

"I can't think of anything more upsetting to a child's sense of well-being than to say that he or she might not be with his or her parents," says Blankenhorn. "You can't frighten a child more than that."

"The human newborn is one of the most helpless creatures on earth," wrote Judith Wallerstein in *Second Chances: Men, Women and Children a Decade After Divorce.* "Human children need their parents far longer than any other animal species, and children are tragically aware of this fact . . . Accordingly, they have a very primitive, very real fear of being left on their own . . . When their family breaks up, children fear that their lifeline is in danger of being cut. Their sense of sadness and loss is profound. A five-year-old enters my office and talks about divorce with the comment 'I've come to talk about death.' Children grieve over the loss of the family, the loss of the parent who has left home, and the imagined loss of both parents.''

Today, more children are receiving psychiatric counseling — juvenile mental health has become one of the fastest-growing areas of medicine — and rates of juvenile delinquency, drug abuse, alcoholism, anorexia, obesity, depression, and suicide are at extraordinarily high levels, and increasing. The Institute of Medicine estimates that as many as 7.5 million children — 12 percent of those below the age of eighteen — suffer from some form of psychological illness. A federal survey shows that after remaining constant for ten years, hospitalizations of youngsters with psychiatric disorders jumped from 81,500 to about 112,000 between 1980 and 1986. Since 1960, the suicide rate among those fifteen to nineteen has tripled; the number of suicides has quadrupled, from 475 to 2,059 in 1988. Significantly, the single biggest factor in suicide among the young is the absence of a father.

Children whose parents split up, studies show, are more likely to do poorly in school or to drop out. "The family has primary responsibility for passing on traits of character and competence," says Blankenhorn. "Basically, a child wants two things: one, the unconditional love of his or her biological parents, and two, that his or her parents stay together. When children don't have those things, when the family fails, the result is declining character and competence.

"Ask any first-grade teacher. They'll tell you they're getting children who are less able every year to do what first-graders are supposed to do. The kids don't have social competence, they can't sit still, they can't pay attention, they aren't ready to learn."

In Japan, a largely homogeneous society where social norms are stronger and there is a greater sense of tradition and discipline, less than 1 percent of births occur out of wedlock, and the incidence of divorce is only a third as high as in the United States. The greater degree of family integrity means that all ages share in the Japanese economic boom; the fraction of children living in poverty in Japan fell by 50 percent between 1975 and 1985.

By contrast, younger families and children in the United States are worse off today. For one thing, more fathers are deadbeats, skipping out on their financial obligations to their offspring. When the father is absent, studies show, only 37 percent of children receive child-support payments. After a divorce, fathers typically are better off, and mothers worse off, especially if they have primary responsibility for the care and rearing of children. During the first year after divorce, women with minor children experienced a 73 percent decline in standard of living, a Harvard study found; their husbands enjoyed a 42 percent increase.

The children of single parents are five times as likely to be poor as children born to married couples. From 1970 through 1982, more than two thirds of the increase in the number of children living in poverty was in households headed by women. Today, more than half of all children living in single, female-headed households are impoverished.

In recent years, moreover, there's been a big twist in the age profile of wealth in favor of older people. Since 1974, the poverty rate among children has exceeded that among the elderly, and 40 percent of all poor people in this nation today are children. Between 1978 and 1987, spending on programs for the elderly rose 52 percent; spending on children dropped 4 percent. Nearly a quarter of all children under six live in households that are struggling below the official poverty line — $12,675 a year for a family of four. "We are hypocrites," charges Senator John D. Rockefeller IV, of West Virginia, who is chairman of the National Commission on Children. "We say we love our children, yet they have become the poorest group in America."

"The most telling statistic," says Popenoe, "is that in 1960 the average person spent 62 percent of his adult life with spouse and children, which was the highest in history; today, that figure has dropped to 43 percent, which is the lowest in American history. That's quite a shift. Later marriage, fewer children, more divorce, and greater longevity — all these factors mean people are out of the family circuit much more than ever before. Today, only 38 percent of households contain children. What that means is that there is a huge group of adults with no direct responsibility for children. This shows up politically in less support for schools and children's measures in Congress, and it shows up in higher levels of childhood poverty."

"Under our tax laws," says Representative Pat Schroeder, of Colorado, "a businesswoman can deduct a new Persian rug for her office but can't deduct most of her costs for child care. The deduction for a Thoroughbred horse is greater than that for children."

"We are becoming as a society more and more indifferent to the needs of children," says Blankenhorn. "If you take a hard look at the choices being made, from the bedroom and the kitchen table to the White House, you'll see an unwillingness to make the sacrifices necessary to promote good outcomes for children. As a result, we're setting our society up for a disastrous future."

When sociologists try to explain why the family has fallen apart, they often cite such factors as increased mobility, the birth control pill, the women's movement, the sexual revolution, and the secularization of American society. But the chief culprit is what social scientists call "affective individualism" or "modernist individualism" — which is a turgid way of saying that people today are much more self-centered than in the past.

Marriage — the union that creates the family — and childrearing — the chief business of the family — both require a substantial measure of self-denial and self-sacrifice. Lately, the idea of self-sacrifice has come to seem laughably archaic, especially among urban sophisticates. For too many Americans, that facetious yuppie credo — "He who dies with the most toys wins" — has become a guiding philosophy. The self comes first, and the only shrewd way to live is to amuse and entertain and please the self with as many experiences, sensations, material goods, and fulfilled wishes as possible.

"What has emerged from the cultural shifts of the last twenty-five years," says Popenoe, "is an ethos of radical individualism in which personal autonomy, individual rights, and social equality have gained supremacy as cultural ideals. In keeping with these ideals, the main goals of personal behavior have shifted from obligation and commitment to social units — such as families, communities, religions, and nations — to personal choices, lifestyle options, self-fulfillment, and personal pleasure."

As everyone knows, the nuclear family began to come apart in the 1960s, when the leading edge of the baby-boom generation rebelled against the bland Ozzie-and-Harriet normality of the 1950s. Propelled by raging hormones, a whole cohort of teenagers somehow managed to elevate their adolescent restiveness into a cultural revolution. Under the banner of free love, they celebrated polymorphous perversity and championed an ethos that exhorted, "If it feels good, do it."

Suddenly, self-exploration and self-indulgence were not merely options; they were obligations. As the word itself denoted, the counterculture defined itself less by what it was for than by what it was against: all authority was suspect, anything that smacked of tradition or the Establishment was discredited, and the hoary institution of marriage was rejected as just another ruling-class instrument of oppression. Marriage, charged Kate Millett in *Sexual Politics*, is a tool for perpetuating patriarchal tyranny and confining women "to the cultural level of animal life." Another feminist, Judith Brown, called marriage "an anachronism" that is "oppressive politically, exhausting physically, stereotyped emotionally and sexually, and atrophying intellectually . . . [It] is the atomization of a sex so as to render it politically powerless."

While most women rejected such extreme views, many, observed Christopher Lasch in *The Culture of Narcissism*, began to regard marriage as "the ultimate trap, the ultimate routine in a routinized society, the ultimate expression of the banality that pervades and suffocates modern life."

Who needed marriage (and husbands) now that women were lugging their own briefcases and cashing their own paychecks? Who needed marriage (and wives) now that practically any man could walk into practically any singles bar on any night of the week and, for the price of a few drinks, go home with a bra-less nymphet who would guide him through the *Kamasutra*? It was an era of love, peace, and happiness, fueled in large measure by far-out drugs and no-hassle sex — two popular diversions, according to Lasch, that created "the illusion of intense experience without emotion."

Then came the seventies, and from sea to shining sea everyone was "into" the Self. "My heart belongs to me," sang Barbra Streisand. "There is no Mr. Right," proclaimed the brave new single woman. "There is Mr. *Right Now*." Forget marriage, forget the family, forget the future and death. Different strokes for different folks. I do my thing and you do your thing. I gotta do it my way — or no way at all. I need my space. I am my own work of art. The end product is ME! Marriage, with its demands for sacrifice, compromise, and surrender, hardly had a chance.

There was Mom, her consciousness raised, ditching Dad and the kids so that she could run off with the twenty-five-year-old Bjorn Borg lookalike who was teaching her how to play tennis. And there was Dad, infected by Hugh Hefner's gospel of hedonistic he-manism, suddenly growing sideburns, wearing bellbottoms, pumping iron, driving a fire-engine-red Corvette, and cavorting with what Tom Wolfe called the New Cookie — "the girl in her twenties for whom the American male now customarily shucks his wife of two to four decades when the electrolysis gullies appear above her upper lip."

As a child of the 1950s, who came of age in the 1960s and 1970s, I saw much of this unfold at first hand. I remember one experience in particular that for me will always represent the lunacy of that period. In 1970 or thereabouts, when I was a student at Princeton, I got a call from an alumnus for whom I had worked when I was in high school. He and his wife were chartering a bus, he said, to bring a bunch of friends up to Princeton for a football game, and he wanted to know whether I'd be willing to serve as bartender during a private party at his old eating club.

I readily agreed, and sure enough, on the appointed Saturday, the group arrived. It was a young, monied, classy crowd, the beautiful people of the Philadelphia Main Line, effervescent, successful couples whom life had denied nothing, the kind of people John Cheever or John Updike might easily have woven a short story around — handsome, athletic men with crisp haircuts and taut physiques, wearing tasteful tweeds and rep ties, smooth-skinned women with vanilla-blond pageboys, strong backhands, and the carefree laugh of the privileged.

There had been a lot of drinking on the bus ride up, there was a lot of drinking before, during, and after the game, and there was a lot of drinking, apparently, on the bus ride home. Naturally, as the group's spirits rose, their inhibitions fell.

79

Soon, there was some flirting, and some necking, and some serious propositioning. Several spousal arrangements were realigned, and assignations were set. Afterward, some of the dalliances begun on that bus ride developed into full-fledged affairs. I later learned that many couples who took that trip eventually got divorced, several because of the entangling alliances initiated on that fateful day.

Looking back on that episode, I'm more inclined to blame the Zeitgeist, the unrestrained, anything-goes temper of the times, than the people. They were basically good, solid, churchgoing, contributing citizens determined to do the right thing, but they were seduced by the sudden glorification of permissiveness into believing that the trendy thing to do — the thing that everybody else was doing — was to jeopardize their marriages and their families and their children's welfare for the momentary thrills of romantic adventure and sexual self-indulgence.

At any rate, the broken marriages caused by that single Princeton football outing added only more weight to a veritable avalanche of divorce that was smashing the American family. In 1974, for the first time in American history, more marriages ended in divorce than in death. As the number of divorces more than tripled and the divorce rate more than doubled, marriage was fast becoming, in the words of Gore Vidal, "no more than a ceremonial vestige of a bygone era." The more people got divorced, of course, the more "normal" divorce became, and hence the weaker the sanctions against it.

Meanwhile, the first cohorts of the baby-boom generation, eager to prolong their irresponsible adolescence, terrified of surrendering any personal freedom, were buying condos and shunning matrimony en masse. From 1970 to 1980, the population of unmarried women between twenty-five and twenty-nine doubled, and the number of unmarried couples living together tripled, soaring from 532,000 to 1.5 million. Eventually, some of those cohabitants did tie the knot, but not for very long; between 1960 and the late seventies, the divorce rate for couples under thirty quadrupled.

"Previous generations were taught that life is hard, sacrifice is necessary, and unhappiness a cross that sometimes must be borne," explained Landon Y. Jones in *Great Expectations*. "But the baby boomers were not willing to make the risky and often painful compromises their parents did. Just as they had great expectations for themselves, they had great expectations for their marriages. Life was too short to live with an unhappy marriage. If they could switch to another TV channel, why not switch husbands or wives? In fact, their satisfaction and sense of self-obligation practically demanded it."

In the eighties, the social turmoil seemed to simmer down, largely because the baby boomers, finally growing up and running out of libidinal steam, switched from one vice, lust, to another, greed. Many members of that generation had set out to start a revolution, and in many ways they succeeded. Marriage and the family, for instance, were changed radically, to the real benefit of many adults and the real detriment of many children.

"The earlier social story about marriage," says Blankenhorn, "was that this is a public commitment, a nonbreakable covenant that is legally, morally, and spiritually binding. You are not only pledging something to one another, you are pledging something to the community. Today, marriage is a purely private arrangement made for the fulfillment of individuals and can be terminated at will by either party at any time, and no one is to blame."

Twenty-five years ago, the vast majority of Americans said that couples involved in an unhappy marriage should stay together for the sake of the children. Today, the vast majority says such couples should split — a breathtaking change in public opinion, and yet another illustration of our unwillingness to subordinate personal needs and desires to larger purposes. If you're unhappy with your marriage, you leave it. If you don't want to spend a lot of time with a little child, you don't. It's all part of the shift away from institutional loyalty and toward self-gratification.

"The cultural emphasis on self-fulfillment and self-gratification has resulted in a lowered commitment to relationships of all kinds, including that to spouse and children," says Preston. In 1957 and 1976, years that bracket the period of most rapid family change in American history, a representative sample of Americans were quizzed about their attitudes toward marriage and family. In 1957, when men were asked "How is a man's life changed by being married?", 43 percent gave answers like "You give up your freedom," "You have to think about someone else" — answers that indicated they viewed marriage as restrictive. Nearly twenty years later, the proportion of men who gave restrictive answers to that question rose to 60 percent. Similarly, when asked "How is a man's life changed by having children?", 29 percent of the men in 1957 gave restrictive answers; by 1976, that figure had risen to 45 percent.

At a time when marriage is viewed primarily as a means to self-fulfillment rather than a structure for creating a family and rearing children, it should hardly be surprising that so many fail and break apart. In fact, the probability that a marriage contracted today will end in divorce ranges from 44 percent to 66 percent; of every twenty couples exchanging sweet embraces at the altar, as many as ten, and maybe more, will someday claw their way into court.

"People are withdrawing from family concerns," says Popenoe. "They don't want to get involved because they're afraid to give up their freedom and take the risk. So they are investing in themselves and their own education and advancement. They postpone commitment, they delay marriage, they don't marry, and they don't have kids, because having kids represents an even greater risk.

"Perhaps the most serious problem is a weakening in

many families of the fundamental assumption that children are to be loved and valued at the highest level of priority. The general disinvestment in family life has meant a disinvestment in children's welfare. Some refer to this as a national 'parent deficit.' Yet the deficit goes well beyond parents to encompass a less child-friendly society."

The consequences for children are terrible, because they are essentially vulnerable. They are always at the mercy of society; they cannot promote or defend their own interests. They have no money; they have no vote; they have no political power. They are dependent on their parents and elders and those few advocates who are fighting for public resources on their behalf. But the demographer Preston points out that low fertility and high family breakup weaken the support for children's programs. In the 1982 congressional elections, Preston found that only 38 percent of voters lived in households that contained a child under eighteen. Consequently, many older people are using their political power to skew the nation's laws to their own advantage.

At least in theory, we Americans have great respect for the idea of the family, and obviously there are many Americans who are deeply devoted to their spouses and children and for whom the family comes first. But even among those who have the best of intentions toward their families, there are stresses and strains that make it difficult to be a parent, or at least the kind of parent who succeeds at producing children who will grow up to be citizens of character and competence.

In 1970, 30 percent of mothers with children under the age of six were in the work force. By 1987, this figure had leaped to 57 percent, and the number is expected to keep climbing. Many women are working because they want to, because they want to challenge themselves and fulfill themselves in careers outside the home. But there are many women who work because they *have* to, because they have no choice if they wish to feed and clothe their children, or maintain a semblance of the middle-class standard of living they enjoyed, and perhaps took for granted, while growing up.

"It's important to point out that the mother-child bond is not much weaker than it ever was," says Preston. "It's true that women are working to a greater extent than they used to. But men who want to blame all the problems of the family on the fact that women are working are wrong. The problem lies mainly with the departure of men, with women having to raise kids by themselves, and the departed men not contributing time or money to that arrangement." A large majority of men fail to pay child support; about half of the men who are divorced don't see their children as frequently as once a month; 40 percent don't see them as frequently as once a year. "For a significant number, it's a total writeoff," says Preston, "a total abdication of their responsibilities as fathers."

Regardless of who's to blame, what it all adds up to is that children aren't getting what is perhaps the most important thing parents can provide: time. The amount of "total contact time" between parents and children has dropped 40 percent over the past twenty-five years, says the Family Resource Council in Washington. Gone are the days of the sit-down dinner, when children and adults shared conversation and the experiences of the day. Many parents are too exhausted and frazzled for such family-affirming rituals. More likely, supper comes out of the microwave and is swallowed on the run; afterward, children are parked in front of the television, where they are kept occupied by electronic baby sitters like the VCR or HBO. Parents who feel guilty about spending too little time with their children often spend money instead. And so they shower their kids with Teenage Mutant Ninja Turtles and Nintendo games and Reebok sneakers, inculcating the gospel of consumerism, preparing their children to become mall-cruising materialists.

For many yuppie couples, children are simply another luxury item, living, breathing status symbols to be ferried about in the Volvo station wagon. Preoccupied with their own careers and interests, they entrust their children to nannies and housekeepers, day-care centers and private schools, feeling heroic because they've bought their children the best that money can buy and because they've managed to pause from their hectic bicoastal schedules to bestow upon their blessed progeny an occasional half hour of "quality time."

Not long ago, I talked with James L. Crawford, Jr., the headmaster of the Episcopal Academy, one of the oldest and most prestigious private schools in the Philadelphia area. He was lamenting that today's parents have much higher expectations of the school than those of twenty or even ten years ago. Because parents now are so busy and so focused on their careers and "success," they want — indeed, demand — that the school educate their children academically and athletically and also tend to a panoply of physical, spiritual, emotional, and psychological needs — to function, that is, as a kind of institutional superparent, covering for parents who are simply too busy to be parents.

"In a school like this, we've always seen some parents who spoil their kids, but there's more of it now than I can remember, for different kinds of reasons," Crawford says. "Basically, what a lot of people are doing is treating the symptoms rather than the disease, because they don't have the time or the know-how or they want to avoid unpleasantness.

"There are so many parents today who want the raising of their children to be easy. The idea is that kids are supposed to be enjoyable and you're supposed to go from one good time to the next, and when it doesn't work that way, there's something wrong. And who gets the blame? Well, not themselves. It's the kids or the school or the kids' friends. Some of them take the easy way: give them more, give them more, give them more. We see a lot of that — parents trying to overcome the difficult times by giving, by rewarding. And that clears their conscience. At least they can say, 'My kid had everything he needed.' Of course that can be just the opposite of what *should* be done. It's very hard to say no. It's very hard to punish. But children need discipline, and occasionally punishment, if they're going to grow into healthy, productive, competent adults."

Our society has assigned to the family the crucial task of socializing children — of passing on values, of developing character and competence. We don't tell schools to do it; we don't tell churches or synagogues to do it. We may ask them to reinforce the family in its role, but there is really no backup system. Either the family does the job or it doesn't get done. It is still true that the hand that rocks the cradle rules the world. If that hand falters, if it stops, if it doesn't know how to, if it doesn't know whether it wants to, if it wants to do something else, then our whole society suffers.

The family is cardinal because the family is where youngsters learn the values that will govern their behavior as adults — values like trust and obligation and respect for others. The family is vital in fostering what sociologists call "prosocial behavior" — the behavior of those who go out of their way to help others. "Generally, children who are very prosocial," says Popenoe, "were brought up in homes where the discipline usually took the form of reasoning. The pro-social children were taught to think through the consequences of their actions on others, and thus learned empathy."

The drawback of this mode of discipline is that it requires time, plenty of it. To begin with, parents have to be there. And they have to be able and willing to spend more than a few minutes with the children discussing the implications of their actions. But parents today face such a tremendous time deficit that when it comes to discipline, they are either wholly permissive or they mete out quick punishment without explaining why. Popenoe says, "Children are growing up never learning to think about the impact of their behavior on others. They become self-centered and narcissistic, and as they go, so goes the society."

While the President and other politicians mouth platitudes about the sanctity of the family, those who are actually raising children often feel they receive little credit and support from a society that no longer appreciates their efforts or rewards their sacrifices or understands how crucial stable marriages and strong families are to the nation's welfare.

"There's little attention given to marriage as an important means of preserving and passing on our cultural and religious heritage," says Sally Green, director of education at the Marriage Council of Philadelphia. "There's little hype for marriage as a social or religious contract — a sanctification, a holiness. And if you don't glorify it, if marriage as an institution has no greater meaning, how can you justify a relationship where there's so much giving in and sacrificing? If you're going to ask me to clean up crap from my husband and kids for fifty years, I want to know the greater good. I don't see it out there today. Nobody's clapping their hands."

Until recently, the compliment "good family man" was widely heard in our society, bestowed as a badge of honor. "The rough translation was 'He puts his family first,'" says Blankenhorn. "The word *good* meant he had moral values; the word *family* meant he believed in purposes larger than the self; and the word *man* meant he was fulfilling a norm of masculinity. But today, especially within elite culture, the phrase sounds antiquated, almost embarrassing. Contemporary American culture no longer celebrates a compelling ideal of the man who puts his family first."

Not only are the contributions of good mothers and fathers less honored, but also there's been a deterioration of what sociologists refer to as the "social ecology" of childhood. "Raising children isn't an individual act," wrote the social historian Barbara Dafoe Whitehead in her essay "The Family in an Unfriendly Culture." "It is a social and communal enterprise, involving kin, neighbors, other parents, friends, and many other unrelated adults. Typically, hermits don't raise kids; villages do.

"Some new parents expect to rediscover the 'village' of their childhood, intact and waiting for their own children. But they will soon find that the culture of that time was not as permanent and durable as the Sears swing sets their fathers installed in the back yard. That culture was a fragile social construction, cobbled together by their own parents, who spent years as Little League coaches, Brownie troop leaders, community fundraisers, Sunday School teachers, chauffeurs and chaperons. And . . . this culture has fallen into disrepair and disuse in the last several decades, unappreciated . . . and looked down on as unfashionable by much of official America."

"When you look at the social ecology of childhood," says Blankenhorn, "and by that I mean the nature of the other relationships in a child's life — not just the parent-child relationship but also the relationships to other people in the neighborhood — it's clear that those relationships are deteriorating as community life disintegrates and as the institutions of civil society become frayed. The community environment, the social surround of the family, is seen as hostile to the goals of family life."

The consequences are already evident.

Evident in the fact that as many as 30 percent of infants eighteen months and younger are suffering from such psychological ailments as emotional withdrawal and anxiety attacks.

Evident in the epidemic of violent crime by kids who sometimes aren't yet teenagers, horrible acts of antisocial fury committed without the slightest trace of remorse. "Children who go unheeded," warns the Harvard psychiatrist Robert

Coles, "are children who are going to turn on the world that neglected them."

Evident, too, in the attitudes and behavior of those forty-eight million young Americans between the ages of eighteen and twenty-nine who fall between the baby boomers and the boomlet of children the baby boomers are producing. In a disturbing cover story, *Time* recently profiled that generation — a generation that grew up in a time of drugs, divorce, and economic strain and virtually reared themselves — and portrayed it as cautious, passive, paralyzed, passionless, and eager to avoid risk, pain, and rapid change. "What worries parents, teachers, and employers," *Time* noted, "is that the latest crop of adults wants to postpone growing up."

Many of those children were latchkey kids, the first to experience the downside of the two-income family. Left to fend for themselves, they felt lonely and neglected, and today they are resentful of their absentee parents and contemptuous of "quality time," which they feel they never had much of. An estimated 40 percent of people in their twenties are children of divorce, and this too has taken its toll; many are afraid of commitment and highly skeptical about marriage. Studying those twenty to twenty-four in 1988, the U.S. Census Bureau found that 77 percent of men and 61 percent of women had never married, up sharply from 55 percent and 36 percent, respectively, in 1970. Among those twenty-five to twenty-nine, the unmarrieds include 43 percent of men and 29 percent of women in 1988, contrasted to 19 percent and 10 percent in 1970. Clearly, this is a generation that is paying the price for the sexual experimentation and voluptuous excesses of its parents. It is a generation that has elevated casual commitment to an art form, a generation too detached to form caring relationships, a generation that is afraid to undertake the challenge and responsibility of our most essential human mission: forming a family and raising children.

"The main effect of the modernist individualism that

we've seen in the last twenty-five years, and that, in the extreme, tends toward gross irresponsibility and narcissism, is a pulling away from obligation and commitment to others," says Popenoe. "People still maintain a vague commitment to society and abstract ideals like peace and a clean environment, but the nitty-gritty of society is, and must be, obligation and commitment to others — families, neighborhoods, and community. That's what society is built on."

When his own marriage broke up, the novelist Pat Conroy observed, "Each divorce is the death of a small civilization." Indeed, that is what the family is — a small civilization, society in microcosm. And if the family is sick, if the family falls apart and fails to function, it's only a matter of time before society as a whole becomes ill and begins to decline. "Every society faces the task of civilizing an onrushing horde of barbarians — its own children," my grandfather is fond of saying. That proverb is probably truer today than ever (particularly with regard to the word *barbarians*), but the American family, I fear, is no longer capable of performing that urgent task. Already, the consequences are upon us — and, tragically, sure to get worse.

5 The Decline of Education

A teacher at a public elementary school:
"The incompetence is incredible. A lot of teachers simply can't teach; they just don't know the material. A second-grade teacher at my school came up to me and asked me, 'How many weeks in a year?' I couldn't believe it. I said, 'Fifty-two.' She said, 'How did you know that?' I said, 'I learned it in elementary school.' Then she asked me how many days in a year. She truly did not know. And this is a person who is going to be teaching.

"Many of the teachers can't teach because they don't know the basic content. How can you teach vowel sounds, fractions, and polar coordinates if you don't know that stuff yourself? Some of the teachers are threatened by the curriculum because it's just too difficult for them. In sixth grade, they're supposed to teach the kids about electricity, magnetism, and circuitry, and they simply don't teach it because they're afraid to.

"Some of them just don't have it. I see it every day in committee meetings. I can tell by the look in their eyes and on their faces that they don't get it, that they're not following my train of thought. A majority don't read; they don't know what's going on in the world. And what they're hiring now just gets worse and worse. The girl who teaches in the classroom next to me had to take the school district qualifying test four times to pass it.

"A sixth-grade math teacher didn't know place values.

A whole batch of math tests were marked wrong because the teacher didn't know the right answers. Another teacher at my school couldn't teach relative position because she was confused about it. She couldn't remember the six basic directions — right, left, front, back, above, below. She was even confused about right and left. The kids got it before she did.

"*One teacher in the intermediate grades was complaining that her children didn't do well on a test she had given them on proper adjectives. When I looked at the test, I was amazed to discover that she wanted them to recognize* chester *drawers as a proper adjective when what she meant was* chest *of drawers. A primary teacher recently complained about the use of nonsense words to test children in phonics. The 'nonsense' words she was referring to were* spew *and* yew. *I had to pull out a dictionary and show her that these were indeed real words . . .*

"*The thing I resent the most is that the few of us who do do our jobs get dumped on. If there are discipline problems that another teacher can't handle, they put those kids in our classrooms. We're supposed to turn in lesson plans. Many teachers don't bother, and nothing happens to them.*

"*It just goes on and on, and you get to a point where you close the classroom door and do your job and pray that whatever's happening around you doesn't directly affect you. If there's a brawl in the hall, you ignore it and keep on teaching. Let someone else worry about it. It almost doesn't pay to be a professional and do the job right, because you just get dumped on.*"

I N 1983, the U.S. Department of Education, declaring that America was a "nation at risk," released a report on the dismal state of education in this country and warned that the foundations of our society were being eroded by "a rising tide of mediocrity that threatens our very future as a nation and a people." The report continued: "If an unfriendly foreign power had attempted to impose on America the mediocre educational performance that exists today, we might well have viewed it as an act of war."

Since then, many states have poured more money into schools, revamped programs, raised teacher salaries, and toughened graduation requirements.

The results?

Zip.

In 1990, the U.S. Department of Education announced that the reading and writing skills of the nation's students have remained virtually unchanged and show signs of declining in the decade ahead. "Frankly, there has been very little education progress made in the United States," said former Education Secretary Lauro F. Cavazos, who termed the reading and writing skills of U.S. students "dreadfully inadequate."

Despite a steady increase in education funding — it rose from $185 billion in 1986 to $199 billion in 1990 — college entrance exam scores and the dropout rate of high school students have continued to worsen. "Anything would be better than what we're doing now," said Cavazos. "We have reached a plateau."

Just how abysmal is American education?

▶ *Only 42 percent of seventeen-year-old high school students are adept enough at reading to comprehend a newspaper editorial or a twelfth-grade textbook.*

▶ *Only 6 percent can compute simple interest.*

▶ *Only 26 percent can spot Greece on a world map.*

▶ *Many high school seniors do not know who Winston Churchill was or what happened in 1914.*

▶ At one Chicago high school, only 10 percent of the entering tenth-graders could read effectively.

▶ In Houston, a geometry teacher assigned a problem requiring students to find a proof. Only 2 of 110 students were able to solve it.

▶ In New York City, at academic high schools geared to prepare students for college, one of every five students is absent on any given day. In four of those schools, the absence rate approaches one in three.

▶ Each year, almost 700,000 students call it quits — a group larger than the population of Boston. In New York, at least one of every three students drops out; at one high school in Los Angeles, seven out of ten students leave between the ninth and twelfth grades.

▶ In Chicago, on an average day, about 5700 children in 190 classrooms come to school to find they have no teacher because the system cannot afford enough substitutes.

▶ New York City's school buildings are so old and dilapidated that it would cost $4.2 billion over the next ten years to refurbish them.

▶ From 1969 to 1990, the combined average SAT score for college-bound seniors fell fifty-six points.

"We have public education at the elementary and secondary level that ranks below every industrial competitor we have in the world," says former Labor Secretary William

Brock. Albert Shanker, the president of the American Federation of Teachers, warns, "We cannot survive as a country continuing as we are going."

For many children, the education deficit begins in the womb. More than 30 percent of pregnant mothers receive inadequate prenatal care. Many mothers smoke or drink or take crack during pregnancy, starving their children of essential nutrients, stunting their growth, condemning them to lifelong physical, intellectual, and emotional handicaps — if they survive infancy. Nearly forty thousand babies born in the United States each year die before their first birthday; at least 250,000 babies are born seriously underweight. To keep these infants in intensive care costs about $3000 a day, and such children are two to three times more likely to be blind, deaf, or mentally retarded.

More than 20 percent of America's children are undernourished; half a million suffer from malnutrition. "Of all the dumb ways of saving money, not feeding pregnant women and kids is the dumbest," says Dr. Jean Mayer, the president of Tufts University and one of the world's leading experts on nutrition. During the first year of life, a child's brain grows to two-thirds its final size. Babies denied healthful food during this critical period later need intensive nutritional and developmental therapies to repair the damage.

Because so many parents work, many toddlers and preschoolers are entrusted to baby sitters or deposited at day-care centers. Some are wonderful, but too many are mediocre or worse. Even for the most affluent and well connected, finding competent, reliable child care today is chancy, difficult, and expensive. For those with limited resources, frustration can lead to desperate measures, such as leaving children at home, alone, shut up in a room all day. After firing three baby sitters who had stolen her food, invited guests to her home, and left her five-year-old daughter unattended, a divorced woman from Elizabeth, New Jersey, locked her child in her car trunk while she worked on the weekends at a shopping mall.

More often, busy mothers and fathers, from the underclass to the upper class, park their children in front of the television set. "It starts in childhood," says the sociologist Amitai Etzioni. "Often, the parents are not at home and the kids are brought up on TV. It's their first strong influence in life. Instead of some kind of discipline or structured guidance, they have this junk food of the mind."

"The average child sits in front of the TV four hours a day, seven days a week," says Robert Eisenberger, a psychology professor at the University of Delaware. "It gets them used to doing nothing and creates a flightiness of attention. TV shows, in order to attract attention, have very rapid changes in scene and story line. To compete, teachers are imitating this technique, jumping from one topic to another after a very few minutes."

Watching television is by far our most popular national pastime, perhaps because it requires less skill to gaze at the tube than it does even to eat. "More Americans now have television sets than have refrigerators or indoor plumbing," wrote the psychologists Robert Kubey of Rutgers University and Mihaly Csikszentmihalyi of the University of Chicago in *Television and the Quality of Life: How Viewing Shapes Everyday Experience.* "The medium has clearly become an American institution, substantially altering and influencing every other institution and ranking with the family, the school, and the church as contemporary culture's prime forces of socialization."

On average, we Americans commune with the sacred electronic box two hours a day — the equivalent of seven years during the course of a lifetime. For many children, for better or worse, it is the most powerful influence in their lives. The average child will have watched five thousand hours of TV by the time he enters first grade and nineteen thousand hours by the end of high school — more time than he will spend in class. "Children who have grown up goggle-eyed around the electric altar cannot believe that anything is real unless it comes with a laugh track," wrote Pico Iyer in *Time*. "They organize their emotions around commercial breaks and hope to heal their sorrows with a PAUSE button. Watching their parents fight, they sit back and wait in silence for the credits. History for them means syndication; ancient history, the original version of *The Brady Bunch*."

In perhaps the most comprehensive attempt to understand what happens to people before, during, and after watching television — a project that involved twelve hundred subjects in nine studies during thirteen years — Kubey and Csikszentmihalyi found that television, more than any other leisure activity, is likely to make people passive, tense, and incapable of concentrating. The longer people watch TV, the more drowsy and bored they become. As time goes on, they grow sadder, lonelier, more irritable, and more hostile. Although it is true that people are relaxed while the television set is on, when they turn it off, they are even less relaxed than before they began to watch.

Such a "co-parent" is hardly ideal for kids, the eminent virtues of *Sesame Street* and *Mr. Rogers' Neighborhood* notwithstanding. By the time they enter kindergarten or first grade, many children are so accustomed to the visual over-stimulation and hyperkinetic pace of television that they are unable to focus, particularly when they're called on to undertake a learning task. For these television-reared children — nervous, jumpy, impulsive — school can't compete; it is too poky, dull, and taxing, no matter how skillful and imaginative the teacher.

For many teachers, however, dealing with "vidkids" is the least of their problems. Because of parental neglect, many children show up for school hungry and inadequately dressed, and the teachers themselves scramble to provide food and clothing, eyeglasses and medical care, sometimes spending money out of their own pockets. Some children receive absolutely no training or educational support at home. "Kids grow up with little interest in school," says Everett J. Williams, the school superintendent in New Orleans. "They come to school not able to count to ten, not knowing their colors, not knowing where they live, and some not even knowing their names. At the beginning of their careers in school, they are already students at risk."

When the monthly meeting for parents was held at a junior high school in Los Angeles recently, only a dozen parents showed up; the school's enrollment is eleven hundred. At a high school in New Orleans, which, like others in the city, required parents to pick up their children's report cards, 70 percent of the cards remained unclaimed two months after the end of the marking period. A first-grade teacher at an elementary school in Cleveland says: "You send notices home, there's no response. You ask parents to come to conferences, they don't come. You send homework home, you can see the parents aren't paying attention to it. They aren't helping their kids." Little wonder so many teachers burn out and give up.

Fortunately, there are still many intelligent, devoted teachers laboring to exhaustion under awful conditions, acting not just as teachers, but as surrogate parents, counselors, and social workers. Unfortunately, there are also far too many teachers who, instead of being the best and the brightest, are the worst and the dimmest. Because of low pay and prestige and better career opportunities in other professions, teaching has fallen on hard times. In recent years, those entering the profession have scored significantly lower than the national average on aptitude tests, and have generally come from the bottom half of their class. Brighter teachers are likely to leave the profession; the dumbest are likely to stay. And studies show there's only one factor that consistently boosts students' academic achievement: the intelligence of the teacher.

In other words, we've entrusted the responsibility for producing tomorrow's competent workers and citizens to a profession that harbors some of the least competent — and some of the most lazy. Many people become teachers, the old saw goes, for three reasons — June, July, and August — and also because the job is secure, largely free from accountability, and, if not taken seriously, relatively easy. To make matters worse, many teachers-to-be spend their college years majoring in education — instead of getting one. According to John Silber, the president of Boston University, the main business of many colleges and schools of education is "certifying the ineducable to be educators" with a curriculum that amounts to "a two- or three-year negative intelligence test."

The Council on Competitiveness, a Washington-based group whose leadership includes representatives of business, labor, and education, estimates that sixty thousand high school math and science teachers are unqualified to teach those subjects. And because of these lousy teachers, many students are so woefully unprepared, they cannot consider technical careers when and if they get to college.

Once entrenched, incompetent teachers are difficult to root out. Because of union protections, firing an inept teacher is a prolonged and costly process. As a result, many districts wind up "passing the trash," transferring incompetent teachers to positions where they'll do the least harm. Meanwhile, students suffer, and taxpayers get gypped.

In the mid-1970s, I was a reporter at a suburban newspaper in Bucks County, Pennsylvania. One of my responsibilities was covering a large suburban school district. Though I did meet several teachers who were energetic and eager to do a good job, I was disappointed, and sometimes amazed, by the low character and incompetence of many of the so-called professionals charged with educating the young in this comfortable, middle-class community.

Several teachers seemed to be refugees from the counter-culture — shiftless, unmotivated, disgruntled ex-hippies, slovenly in dress, slovenly in mind, too stupid or indolent to perform real work in the real world. Others were clearly hackers and bozos, grown-up class clowns and wiseguys who'd obviously drifted into teaching because they could still be lifeguards and beach boys during the summer, and during the school year they'd be "outahere" by three in the afternoon. A math teacher I met struck me as a genuine cretin, only a few brain cells above lapsing into drooling imbecility. He may have been a whiz at trigonometry (though I doubt it), but he was unable to form a complete sentence or follow a linear train of thought. Within the space of a five-minute conversation, he stammered out a lot of loony nonsense that, in retrospect I realized, was a bizarre attempt to convert me to born-again Christianity. I could only pity his captive students.

The superintendent was always designing flow charts and spewing out educationese about "goals and objectives." In our conversations, he rarely mentioned children. He had surrounded himself with a covey of sycophants and flunkies who attempted to justify their existence by churning out abstract reports and surveys and impenetrable longitudinal analyses of curricula. Many of the administrators and "coordinators" and department heads held advanced degrees from state teachers' colleges. To talk to them was to realize that studying education does not mean you're educated, and being educated does not mean you're smart. When these petty bureaucrats were not having long lunches at the local country club to formulate "strategic plans," they were devising all sorts of new forms and regulations and requirements, the main effect of which was to generate more paperwork and to make the lives of teachers more difficult and miserable.

That was fifteen years ago. Perhaps the situation in that school district has improved. Perhaps some of the lunkheads have retired or been replaced by people truly interested in enriching the intellectual lives of children. It is a pleasant hope. The reality, however, is probably far less encouraging. The incompetent teachers undoubtedly are still there because they have every reason to stay, and the bureaucracy, I'm sure, has done what all bureaucracies are programmed to do: grow larger, more complex, and more extraneous to the real mission at hand — in this case, teaching children.

In the early sixties, when Martin Mayer wrote *The Schools*, he discovered that there were more school administrators in New York City than in all of France and more in New York State than in the whole of Western Europe. "Many, many of the nation's school systems have by now gone the same way — and just as many businesses are going the other way," says Albert Shanker. "In some large companies today, there's one manager at headquarters for every five thousand employees. But in many of our large school districts, there's an average of 560 students per administrator, which probably translates into one administrator for every sixteen to twenty teachers!"

William Brock, in a recent interview, said, "I don't know of an industry that spends less money on research and development [than does education]. It is not for lack of money. It is a lack of intelligence and will and competence. It is a bureaucratic inertia that is unbelievable and inexcusable. Between thirty-eight cents and forty-one cents of our education dollar gets to the classroom. That is an act of irrationality. We are not putting our resources where the kids are."

"Our schools operate as command economies," says Shanker. "Incentives, where they exist at all, are lined up the wrong way. People in schools are not rewarded for improving student outcomes. They're rewarded for following a bunch of routines — such as handing in attendance registers on time or following a lesson plan — that have little to do with the success of the school as an educational institution."

"The job appears somewhere between a joke and an impossibility," complained one New York City principal to the Carnegie Foundation for the Advancement of Teaching. "The staff and I are directed instantly to implement new programs to resolve current social crises, to use the latest research on teaching, to tighten supervision, increase consultation, and to report back in detail on all the above. There are pages of new rules and regulations to study: it would take a few months to make sense of the Regents plan alone. Responding to it would take a lifetime. Meanwhile, finding the funds to buy paper, repair our single rented typewriter, fix a computer, or tune the piano requires most of my time and imagination."

In many city high schools, teachers have no permanent classroom, or even a desk of their own. The buildings resemble fortresses or prisons. Paint and plaster are flaking off the ceilings, the walls are covered with graffiti, the floors are dirty, the windows grimy, and the rest rooms are a disaster. "I sometimes wonder how we're able to teach at all," says one teacher. "A lot of times there aren't enough textbooks to go around; the library here is totally inadequate; and the science teachers complain that the labs aren't equipped and are out of date. We're always running short of supplies. Last year, we were out of mimeograph paper for a month, and once we even ran out of chalk."

There are, of course, superintendents and administrators who are serious about their responsibilities, know what's wrong with schools today, and are sincerely trying to make them better. But often, for all the power they supposedly wield, they face tremendous obstacles and frustrations, largely because of politics, institutional intransigence, and ridiculous concessions to unions. Today, the New York City school system has nearly a thousand principals, and they, like the teachers, are unionized. Recently, the chancellor of schools negotiated with the principals' union and won back what was hailed on the front page of the *New York Times* as a major victory: the right to remove incompetent principals from their schools.

How and why, you may be wondering, was such a right, so basic to the rational management of a school system, surrendered in the first place? It seems that in 1975, Governor Hugh Carey, grateful for the support of the principals' union in his election campaign, said thank you by muscling the state legislature into passing a law that bestowed upon principals an unbelievable gift: protection from involuntary transfers. In other words, principals gained tenure not only in their schools but also in their assigned buildings! — a prerogative, notes Chancellor Joseph A. Fernandez, enjoyed by principals in no other school system "on the planet." The effect of all this was to make it practically impossible to yank incompetent principals out of schools where they were causing serious damage. Needless to say, without the ability to move around middle managers, the administration found it equally impossible to improve and reform the school system.

Not that all "reform" has been beneficial. The educational establishment, in its zeal to remedy the manifest shortcomings of America's schools, has too often and too hastily embraced the latest fads, only to discover that the old ways weren't so bad after all. At my son's elementary school — a school I attended for two years — a major reconstruction project was recently completed. One of the purposes of the project was to rebuild most of the walls torn down a decade ago to create "open classrooms" — then the hot trend in education. As it turned out, the open classrooms proved too noisy and distracting and were hindering rather than fostering learning.

There was a time when education meant discipline. It was both the aim and essence of the process. The teacher was an undisputed authority figure, a respected role model who guided receptive, conscientious students to enlightenment and, occasionally, wisdom. Now, there is a different relationship between teachers and pupils. Ernest Boyer, in *High School: A Report on Secondary Education in America*, reported, "There is a kind of unwritten, unspoken contract between the teachers and the students: Keep off my back and I'll keep off yours."

"I'm not receiving the same positive response from my students," lamented a teacher interviewed by the Carnegie Foundation for the Advancement of Teaching. "In the past, I felt more like a coach to my students, helping them achieve the highest level of skills they're capable of. But I've felt more in an adversarial position recently, and I don't know why. It's almost as if they say, 'I defy you to teach me.' I had one class of students last year with a dozen chronic behavior problems. I dreaded dealing with that class every day. It affected my whole life."

Ideally, education should accomplish what the Roman poet Horace described as the goal of poetry: to delight and to teach. But nowadays, it seems, too much emphasis is being placed on "delighting." The prevailing attitude — so universally embraced that it's become an axiom of the profession — is that education should be *fun*. And so today's "students" — jaded by video sensation, their attention spans reduced to nanoseconds by the stroboscopic images of MTV — are showered with entertaining, often frivolous electives. One West Coast suburban high school offers its students a smorgasbord of 247 curriculum choices, ranging from Shakespeare and Advanced Chemistry to Consumer Auto, Tots and Toddlers, Wilderness Survival, Gourmet Cuisine, Money Management, Baja Whalewatch, and Bowling.

Too many American students, apathetic, alienated, slothful, are avoiding tough courses like physics and calculus and are taking simplified general education courses. "The majority of students will try at the beginning of the year, but they get a few pages into the work and find that it's too hard," says an English teacher in Chicago. "So they give up. The best of them, even though they can read the words, can't understand much beyond the basic plot and are unable to read for any kind of deeper meaning."

In time, even the most ambitious teachers give up, too. Instead of challenging students with questions that provoke stimulating discussion and require them to use their minds, the teachers essentially baby-sit, filling up class time with reading or workbook assignments. According to one study, barely 5 percent of instructional time in schools is spent on direct questioning and less than 1 percent is devoted to open questioning that calls for higher-level student skills beyond memory.

With so many students in their classes, teachers rarely assign essays, compositions, and term papers; reading and correcting them simply take too long. Instead, students are barraged with regular quizzes, usually of the multiple-choice and matching variety — easy-to-grade, quick-hit tests that show whether students have done their homework but do little to exercise their intellectual muscles and foster deeper understanding of the material. As a result, too few students are learning how to think, and because they can't think, they can't write. Even at elite schools, writing skills today are dreadful.

Over the years, I've visited many of the best public and private schools in the Philadelphia area — schools that routinely send flocks of graduates to the nation's top colleges — to talk to students about journalism and writing. I've also read many school newspapers and student essays and compositions. Although I've encountered heartening exceptions, I can say, with assurance and dismay, that most high schoolers have only a rudimentary grasp of how to use the English language effectively, for much of their writing is sloppy, ungrammatical, obscure, disorganized, and pointless.

Exposure to the eloquent use of language is so uncommon today that most students neither know how to write nor know how to talk. I have no scientific evidence to support this, but I'm willing to bet that three out of four American high-schoolers would have a hard time uttering a thought without using the word *like*, as in "like, you know." Indeed, it is rare, in conversation, to hear a teenager speak in complete sentences, let alone paragraphs that have some direction and cohesion. The vocabulary of many young Americans has shrunk to such a degree that they are incapable of describing, with the appropriate adjective, abstract feelings and situations. Instead, in order to express themselves, they resort to bits of self-dramatizing dialogue. For example, instead of saying: "I was desperate and at my wit's end," they'll say: "I was like, you know, like, I totally didn't know what to do." The expectation among this swelling army of the inarticulate is that meaning will be conveyed by inflection, body English, and enthusiasm rather than by cognitive content. *Like, hey dude, cowabunga!*

While today's students may have appallingly anemic communication skills, they seem to have no trouble expressing their disappointment — nay, outrage — when their meager academic accomplishments are not greeted by outpourings of praise from grateful teachers. In high schools and on college campuses, grade inflation is rampant. Says Eisenberger, "Kids today think a B is their right, and an A is a reward for minimal effort." Students are aided and abetted in these expectations by the schools themselves, which too often push along failing students who ought to be flunked. "It's a game we play," says a teacher in Houston. "If we held them all back, the system would get clogged up. So we water down the curriculum and move them along." Thanks to such "social promotions," many high school juniors and seniors are reading and writing and calculating on a third- or fourth-grade level. Parents frequently make matters worse, bitching because their children have too much homework or complaining because a certain teacher grades tough, thus besmirching the sterling transcripts of their little darlings and jeopardizing their chances of getting into Harvard.

In Parkersburg, West Virginia, the principal of Blennerhassett Junior High recently reprimanded a science teacher, Larry Brown, for giving his eighth-grade students too many D's and F's. Ordered to award more A's, B's, and C's, Brown balked and filed a union grievance, claiming that he gives so many D's and F's because most students aren't doing assignments and therefore score poorly on tests and quizzes. On one recent assignment, Brown said, only four students in a class of eighteen turned in their papers, and only one of those was complete.

"I'm not arbitrarily assigning grades," says Brown. "I don't think it's fair to inflate grades. I believe that's shortchanging the children ... Parents and administrators want the students to have good grades, but students and parents don't want students working for those good grades. When we assign a [high] grade to work that's not up to standard, that's lowering the quality."

Poor Larry Brown. He is fighting a losing battle. Even his fellow teachers fault him for being uncompromising. He probably thinks he's a hero, the Lone Ranger of Education, but actually he's closer to Don Quixote, naïvely pursuing an impossible dream. Doesn't he realize that many students today regard school as a joke, a hassle, a "holding pen" that interferes with their pursuit of sex, rock, rap, booze, drugs, or a new carburetor for their Chevy Camaro? "School is a big place where nobody really cares about you," a Chicago high school student told the Carnegie Foundation for the Advancement of Teaching, "and you do what you do to get by — just like on the streets."

"I see chronic absenteeism, disruptive behavior, and nasty attitudes," reports Ronald James, a teacher at Overbrook High School in Philadelphia. "Many of the students I teach behave as if they have no responsibility for their education. It is to be received passively, like a vaccination."

Recently, James taught *Romeo and Juliet* to an eleventh-grade honors class. He spent six weeks "spoonfeeding" the play to his students. After that, he showed them a film of the play, which was followed by two days of review, during which he all but gave the class the test questions and answers. The result? "A significant number failed the test," he says, "and many angrily claimed that the test was 'unfair.' "

James, who is white, has been a well-respected teacher for twenty-two years. For the past eighteen years, he has taught at Overbrook, which is nearly all black. When he wrote about his frustrations in local newspapers, he ignited an explosion of protest. Hundreds of students demonstrated outside the school, accusing James of racism. Many parents voiced outrage that he was allowed to teach their children. Swiftly, the city's black leaders and opinion makers joined the campaign of vilification. In the end, for expressing such honest views, James was threatened with bodily harm. Fearing for his safety, he took extended sick leave and eventually transferred to another school.

It is ominous that many black students believe academic achievement is a white man's game. John Ogbu, a Nigerian-born anthropologist at the University of California, has found that many blacks equate success in school with "acting white." The disparagement covers speaking standard English, spending a lot of time studying in the library, working hard to get good grades, getting good grades, and being on time — the basic ingredients for academic and professional success.

"It's not as if black children can't do the work, but they don't make the effort," says Ogbu. "The underlying issue for them is one of racial identity. They see doing well in school and getting a high-status job as selling out."

*

Although high school students — white and black alike — may know little about literature and mathematics, they're experts when it comes to their "rights," including the "right" to be promoted and graduated even though they are uneducated, incompetent, and virtually unemployable. "One of the worst things is that the kids in our public school system have due-process rights over their teachers," says Digby Baltzell, the retired University of Pennsylvania sociologist. "And the teachers have no authority over the kids, and the principal has no authority over the teachers. What kind of people are they going to be? How can they be responsible for good work if they're automatically promoted?"

As it is, over a quarter of the nation's youth never finish high school. With no diploma and few skills, they cast about for menial, minimum-wage work, serving Whoppers at Burger King, mopping up floors at McDonald's. Those of a more entrepreneurial bent may wind up peddling coke, eventually becoming neighborhood pharmaceutical tycoons — until they're busted by the narcs or blown away by rival ghetto capitalists.

Either way, it's a hard life that only perpetuates the cycle of ignorance and poverty. "We have not dignified the alternatives to college," said Brock. "We are the only country in the industrial world that says to one of every four of its young people: We are going to let you drop out of sight; we are not going to give you the tools to be productive. No wonder they drop out; the market signal says to them: We don't care about you, so leave school. If you haven't got anything, four dollars an hour sounds like a lot of money. The trouble is that they are still making four dollars an hour when they are thirty, and then they cannot feed and clothe their own children."

By the year 2000, more than half the new jobs will require not only a high school diploma but also some form of postsecondary education. "Employers in both large and small businesses decry the lack of preparation for work among the nation's high school graduates," declared a report by the Council on Economic Development, a business group. "Too many students lack reading, writing, and mathematical skills, positive attitudes toward work, and appropriate behavior on the job. Nor have they learned how to learn, how to solve problems, make decisions, or set priorities. Many high school graduates are virtually unemployable, even at today's minimum wage."

Already, the failures of American education are causing seismic shocks in the job market. David T. Kearns, U.S. deputy secretary of education and former chairman of the Xerox Corporation, calls it "the making of a national disaster." James E. Burke, the chief executive officer of Johnson & Johnson, says it is "the American Dream turned nightmare."

What they are seeing is employees who can't plot numbers on a graph, who cause machine breakdowns because they can't read operating instructions. Major companies like Motorola, Ford, Xerox, Polaroid, and Eastman Kodak are spending millions of dollars a year on basic reading and arithmetical instruction because America's schools have fumbled the ball. Already, it seems, America is developing into a nation of educational haves and have-nots, who are fast becoming employment haves and have-nots.

The problem is double-edged: many workers are less competent, and many of today's jobs demand workers who are *more* competent. Experts, using a jargon of their own, call it "the upskilling" of American industry. As companies invest in automation and new technology, such as robots and computer-aided machinery, they want workers who can read and can think on their feet. Arnold Packer of the Hudson Institute, co-author of *Workforce 2000: Work and Workers for the 21st Century*, says, "It used to be that you could go to work in a steel mill or an auto plant and make a decent living, and the company didn't want you to think very much. Today, that's all changed. Most of the jobs require much more in the way of cognitive skills."

Clearly, not everyone is academically inclined. Not everyone can, and not everyone should, go to college. But today, our society has so depreciated manual labor and practical skills (if you're too dumb to work with your head, you work with your hands), and employers are so obsessed with degrees and credentials, that there is little support and encouragement for those who might lead productive, fulfilling lives as plumbers and electricians, carpenters and machinists, farmers and mechanics. The irony is that a college education is no guarantee of vocational success and happiness; many graduates of our nation's finest colleges and universities are slaving away in mind-numbing, paper-shuffling, white-collar jobs that afford little sense of accomplishment and aren't a fraction as creative and satisfying as building a stone wall, framing a house, or repairing a transmission.

It's all a reflection of a society more interested in making deals than making goods — a trend illustrated by the decline of the comprehensive high school. James B. Conant, a former Harvard University president, was a great proponent of the comprehensive high school, which he described as a "school whose programs correspond to the educational needs of all the youth." In his view, a comprehensive high school should do three things: furnish a general education for students as future citizens (everybody); offer elective programs for students in specialized skills (a majority); and provide advanced academic programs for college-bound students (a minority).

Today, comprehensive high schools in many of our nation's cities are all but dead — or gravely ill. They have been gutted of teachers and programs, robbed of the brightest students, and stripped of their community ties. They've become, in short, the schools for the poor and the poor in spirit. Consider the changes, for example, at John Bartram High School in Philadelphia, one of twenty-two comprehensive high schools in the city. Twenty years ago, Bartram had seventeen shop teachers; today it has four. The print shop is gone. So are the metal shop, machine shop, auto body shop, and a sewing class.

"Somewhere along the way, the word *skills* became a dirty word," observed Larry Moyer, a Bartram English teacher, in a column published in the *Philadelphia Inquirer.* "A plumber became someone with his arm plunged up to his elbow in a toilet, a printer became a shuffling old man in a smudged canvas apron, and a vocational school became a dead-end work camp for students who just couldn't make it in higher education. In our euphoric rush to greet the high-tech society and the service economy, we scarcely noticed the death of 'hands-on learning.' Now, rigor mortis has set in."

What about the kids who do graduate and go on to "higher education"? For one thing, they're not as smart as they — or their parents — think they are. According to literacy studies by the National Assessment of Educational Progress, fewer than 5 percent of American high school graduates would meet the entrance standards of European universities. "We're sending 55 percent of our high school graduates on to college, and 90 percent of these couldn't get into college [in other countries]," says Shanker.

Even America's best students fail to measure up. For example, when the most able math students were tested in Hungary, Scotland, Canada, Finland, Sweden, Japan, New Zealand, Belgium, England, Israel, and the United States, our brainiest high schoolers scored the lowest in algebra and were among the lowest in calculus. Furthermore, our "advanced" science students, the Educational Testing Service reported, ranked last in biology and performed behind students from most countries in chemistry and physics.

Not surprisingly, Japanese students are at or near the top. In college-prep math, in fact, average Japanese students did better than the top 5 percent of U.S. students. Japan has the highest rate of high school completion and literacy in the world, close to 100 percent. Japanese students study more and learn more. They spend more time in class than their American counterparts (their school year is 240 days; ours, 180), they work hard and they are disciplined. What's more, researchers from the University of Michigan have found that Japanese teachers devote most of their classroom time to *teaching* (rather than presiding over vague discussions), and many teach with surprising verve and theatrical flair, using plenty of concrete examples and real-life applications. The result? By the time Japanese students leave high school, they have completed the equivalent of two years at a good American college and are capable of performing technical work that is beyond the powers of most of their U.S. peers. Recently, a Japanese semiconductor company that opened a plant in the southeastern United States had to hire American college students at the *graduate* level to perform statistical quality-control functions. In Japan, the same jobs are handled by high school students.

America's colleges and universities are rightly regarded as the best in the world. But increasingly there's a question as to whether the higher education industry is indeed concerned with education and whether much of that education is any longer "higher."

Of the more than twelve million students enrolled at the nation's colleges and universities each year, a growing number need remedial reading and writing courses, which about two thirds of the colleges now provide. Overrun by hordes of diploma-bearing ignoramuses, professors are reluctantly teaching freshmen and sophomores what they should have learned in high school. "The majority of them are grossly underprepared for coping with college-level academic study," says a professor at a liberal arts institution. "In general, their powers of concentration are poor, their cultural literacy is poor, their scientific and technological literacy is poor, and their capacity for logical thinking, analysis, and synthesis has not been properly developed."

Unfortunately, what the students need most — good teaching — seems to interest fewer and fewer professors, many of whom would rather present a paper at a national convention than lecture to undergraduates. Contemporary academic culture "is not merely indifferent to teaching, *it is actively hostile to it,*" declared Charles J. Sykes, the author of *ProfScam: Professors and the Demise of Higher Education.* "The modern academic is mobile, self-interested, and without loyalty to institutions or the values of liberal education. The rogue professors of today are not merely obscurantists. They are politicians and entrepreneurs who fiercely protect their turf and shrewdly hustle research cash while they peddle their talents to rival universities, businesses, foundations, or government."

At many universities, teaching is a minor factor in promotion decisions; professors who are effective, popular teachers are often penalized at tenure time because of the assumption that anyone putting that much energy into teaching can't be putting enough into research. The stories are legion of promising assistant professors who were superb teachers — outstanding enough, in some cases, to win awards for teaching — who were later punished by being denied tenure. The attitude among senior faculty members, says a former associate professor at Stanford quoted by Sykes, is that "if you're a good teacher, you're not a serious scholar, that they're somehow incompatible." An assistant professor at Yale says, "It would definitely be suicide to be a teacher as a junior faculty member."

Sadly, the days of the kindly, learned professor — the absent-minded scholar who wore rumpled tweeds and droopy bow ties and whose monastic dedication to the pursuit of knowledge made him sage and profound — are plainly over. Today's college professors are too often craven windbags and pretentious intellectual masturbators; shallow ideologues whose productivity — what with all the breaks, holidays, vacations, and sabbaticals — is an outrageous joke; arrogant know-it-alls whose pettiness is exceeded only by their knack for vicious contumely; semantic prestidigitators laboring the obvious, exploring the frontiers of the irrelevant, vowing fealty to the truth but forever making love to methodology; narrow-minded specialists in the trivial and inane — *Deconstruction Meets Beowulf!* — spouting hermetic cant, politicized pap, and pseudoscientific humbug. "Tenure was created to protect brilliant men who thought for themselves," says Baltzell. "It's now protecting incompetent men who have no thoughts at all."

When it comes to teaching, college presidents talk a good game: "It is time for us to reaffirm that education — that is, teaching in all its forms — is the primary task," recently proclaimed Donald Kennedy, president of Stanford. But as any campus idiot knows, the road to academic glory is still paved with research and publications. So ambitious academicians shrewdly apply all their cerebral firepower to minimizing their teaching load — the lightness of which is, for many, a point of pride and a symbol of status. "When I was a professor," says Baltzell, "I taught fifteen hours a week. All of our young people today teach six, right off. Now they come right in and say, No teaching. Why? Because they've got to publish. But do you think they publish any more than we did? Of course they don't."

T. S. Eliot once described the job of a professor as "the elucidation of art and the correction of taste." Many professors today have a far different conception. They see themselves as propagandists, pure and simple. Ostensibly dedicated to "openness" and "diversity," they can be remarkably intolerant and totalitarian toward anything that is not

PC — "politically correct." Some are former hippies who spent the sixties storming the ramparts of the Establishment. Now, twenty years later, these recreational Marxists and weekend communists have become, in effect, tenured radicals. Contemptuous of "the system" (from which they've benefited so handsomely), they reject Western culture, literature, and philosophy because anything Western is, ipso facto, irredeemably racist, sexist, patriarchal, "Eurocentric," and oppressive. They support freedom of speech as long as it doesn't threaten their rosy belief in "multiculturalism" and egalitarianism or interfere with their ability to indoctrinate tractable students with the PC *Weltanschauung*. "If you make any judgment or assessment as to the quality of a work, then somehow you aren't being an intellectual egalitarian," Jean Bethke Elshtain, a political science professor at Vanderbilt, told *Newsweek* recently. Was Shakespeare a whitemale (sic) who didn't write in Swahili? Ban him! Does the word *women* contain the abomination *men?* Then it must be sanitized to *womyn!*

According to the fashionable PC canon, nearly everyone's a victim of some *ism* or another (heterosexism, ageism, lookism, ableism,) perpetrated mainly by "phallocentric," testosterone-poisoned white men. Moreover, everything is freighted with political assumptions and connotations; hence there's no such thing as intrinsic worth or meaning. The best values are no values — which has become a value in itself, the new political and academic orthodoxy. Woe betide those students or fellow professors who disagree or resist. Then the morally smug PC thought police swing into action, calling names, staging protests, interrupting lectures, insinuating evil motives, engaging in all manner of harassment and intimidation until the offending party is "re-educated" and intellectual conformity is restored. Sure, these ideological lynchings by the Sensitivity Gestapo may smack of McCarthyism, but, after all, the ends ("equality," "pluralism," "diversity," "community," and so on) plainly justify the means. So what if many college campuses today seethe with so much tension and resentment — thanks largely to the PC gospel — that they are anything but "communities" and resemble instead hopeless archipelagos of separatist hostility and sanctimony.

The losers are the students. Not only must they endure all the bilge and rot that issue from these pompous visionaries but they must underwrite it as well. For many, the bottom line of higher education is that they're stuck paying as much as $20,000 a year for inaccessible professors, "mass classes" of a thousand or more, and teaching assistants who can't speak intelligible English. At some large universities, it's possible to obtain a bachelor's degree without ever having been taught by a member of the faculty or sitting in a class with fewer than a hundred students. Moreover, distribution requirements are so lax and unfocused that it's possible to graduate without ever performing a laboratory experiment or reading a novel. Posing as bastions of a broad liberal arts education, many colleges and universities are actually glorified vo-tech schools, where middle-class barbarians whose familiarity with Western history, culture, and civilization is limited to what they've gleaned from sitcoms and rock lyrics are permitted to squander their undergraduate years majoring in such horizon-expanding subjects as insurance or fashion merchandising. The curricula at far too many institutions, said the Carnegie Foundation for the Advancement of Teaching in *Campus Life: In Search of Community*, "encourage randomness, not coherence, and create the strong impression that the college has no larger sense of purpose." One student said, "We're kind of like a McUniversity — fast food for the mind."

No wonder so many students fail to take college seriously. No wonder so many view the university as nothing more than a diploma mill, a postadolescent playground to be enjoyed with negligible exertion. According to one study, about one of every four students at four-year institutions say they spend no time in the library during a normal week; 65 percent use the library four hours or less. Says a man familiar with the current crop of college students: "They don't read. They don't even read newspapers except for sports and comics. They are abysmally ignorant of world figures. Mention Albert Schweitzer or Bertrand Russell and they say, 'I didn't take the course.' The talk here is disappointing because they never talk about anything outside their immediate ken. They have no common core of civilized knowledge to draw on. Their conversation is utterly devoid of intellectual curiosity or concern about social problems. They talk only of sports and television, with a little personal gossip. Their knowledge of popular television is astounding."

In June 1990, the Times Mirror Center for the People and the Press issued a report entitled *The Age of Indifference;* it said that today's eighteen-to-thirty-year-olds know less, read less, and care less than any generation in the past five decades. Only 30 percent of Americans under thirty-five said they had "read a newspaper yesterday." That compares with 67 percent of young people who answered the question affirmatively in a 1965 Gallup poll. Respondents between the ages of eighteen and twenty-nine were 20 percent less likely to say they had followed important news stories, and 40 percent less likely to be able to identify a newsmaker like Chancellor Helmut Kohl. The result is a generation that votes less and is less critical of government and business — and is thus an "easy target of opportunity for those seeking to manipulate public opinion," the report warned. "The ultimate irony is that the Information Age has spawned such an uninformed and uninvolved population."

Several months earlier, People for the American Way released a study by the pollster Peter Hart, focusing on fifteen-to-twenty-four-year-olds, that found they were "turned off by politics and tuning out on citizen participation." Asked to define a good citizen, few of those Hart interviewed suggested any civic involvement; only 12 percent even mentioned voting as part of the definition. In a parallel poll, their teachers agreed by a ratio of 2 to 1 that today's high school students have less interest in public affairs than their counterparts in the previous decade.

Ideally, our nation's schools, besides teaching basic academic skills like reading, writing, and arithmetic, should help students develop the ability to think critically; understand the past so that they can deal wisely with the future; prepare for work and further education; gain a spirit of community and service. In all of these areas, however, parents and schools today seem to fall short. By and large, young Americans born in the sixties and seventies are ignorant of their cultural heritage, and unready and unwilling to assume the responsibilities of citizenship.

"Few of the graduates of research universities today have the faintest idea about the Judeo-Christian tradition or the classical heritage from which the very seal on their diploma comes," said James Billington, the Librarian of Congress, in a *U.S. News & World Report* interview. "Today, the research structure in the humanities and social sciences is so attuned to coming up with smart new ways of cutting things apart that no one is putting things back together. If we are going to be together as a people, we have to have a higher-educational process that puts at least a few things back together. Instead, we have a consumer-oriented curriculum that refuses even to make the judgment that Shakespeare is more worth reading than Sartre or that the Bible is more worth knowing than Nietszche."

Our system of government depends on well-educated people who can communicate and express themselves; people who can think and analyze information; people who know what was and are ready for what will be; people who've learned the common culture that binds us as a nation. Without good schools, we won't have good citizens. And without good citizens, we won't have good government. And without good government, today's difficult problems will become tomorrow's impossible tasks.

6 The Decline of the Work Ethic

A former worker at a baking company:

"My nine years at Keebler, which has since shut down, were a period of tears of frustration because of what I saw: lack of dedication, clock-watching, vandalism, stealing, and union protectionism of incompetent people.

"I worked in the lab doing analysis of raw materials, quality control, research and development. I was totally involved in my job, but when I would leave the lab area, a surge of sadness and anger would envelop me because of the attitudes of my fellow workers. The union fought and won often for workers who were drunk, late, had bad work habits, and were thieves. I once spoke against a person who was fired for stealing cookies that were found in his car trunk. My co-workers defended and felt sorry for that person. My feelings were: The rules are there to be obeyed. Needless to say, my opinion was not favorably accepted; my co-workers were on the side of the guilty party, probably because they themselves had engaged in pilfering, but were never caught.

"Yes, I have made mistakes too, but I tried to keep them to a minimum. I have always had pride in my work, whether it was an analysis, filing, or mopping floors. In all my life of working, I have never turned down a job, no matter how menial it was, and I treated them all with importance . . .

"No one age group is responsible for incompetence.

Young and old alike seem to be afflicted with the disease, and I think that's what it is — a disease. It's as though people are saying, 'Everyone has it, so why not me?' The feeling is 'He got away with it, why can't I?'

"Today a lot of people are always blaming the next guy, but did they ever stop and think that they are the next guy? They're blaming the Japanese and everybody else, but did they ever stop and think that when they're putting out a rotten product, they're cutting their own throat? That's exactly what's happening. The American product is basically shoddy because of the lousy attitude of the individual worker, and until we get rid of that, we're in bad trouble."

THE UNITED STATES used to be famous for hard work. Now, *work* has become a four-letter word. Many Americans — whether stuck on an assembly line or in the ranks of middle management — consider work tedious, unsatisfying, a necessary evil that earns the paycheck and buys the food. In a society that idolizes wealth and worships leisure, work is the terrible drudgery that stands between the average American schmo and the weekend. *TGIF! It's Miller Time!*

▸ *The output of a factory is halved on Mondays as many workers call in "sick."*

▸ *Four men from the highway department stand around a pothole, laughing and drinking coffee. Everyone seems to be supervising; no one seems to be working.*

▸ *A sanitation crew squanders the afternoon in a bar when they're supposed to be picking up trash.*

▶ *A policeman spends the bulk of his shift flirting with waitresses and napping in his squad car instead of patrolling the streets.*

▶ *A high-salaried executive whiles away the morning making personal phone calls and reading the paper rather than tending to business.*

Americans no longer believe that work is its own reward. Craftsmanship — and the pride and joy it once inspired — has become extinct. Television bombards us with images of the good life, proselytizing for hedonism. Unions, founded to protect the exploited, now protect the incompetent, sabotaging excellence, demanding more money for less labor. As our productivity sags, our standard of living slips. The proletariat — blue and white collar alike — is surly and disgruntled, and an attitude of entitlement has swept the land. *You owe it to me, man!* In the name of social justice, advocates of affirmative action assail the meritocracy. Suddenly, the American Dream — the possibility of bettering one's life through effort or talent or genius — has ceased to be a promise and is now a right. Somehow, the idea of equality of opportunity has been transmuted into economic parity — equal rewards for all. So why bother to work?

More and more, work engenders frustration, not satisfaction. Automation and computers have stripped work of its humanity, and many service jobs offer no hope of betterment. Noel Cazenave, a sociologist at Temple University, says, "You can't buy a row house working at Roy Rogers." Over the last decade, corporations have become mere commodities, bought and sold by "takeover artists," cannibalized for cash, merged into debt-ridden conglomerates. In the holy name of "restructuring," these megacompanies frequently sacrifice their employees — and quality.

123

In such a predatory atmosphere, many once-loyal middle managers feel anxious and betrayed. Hustling paper in glorified clerical jobs, others are bored and benumbed. Promotions are rare, and many hard-chargers, hitting their career ceilings earlier than expected, are fizzling out as their ambition sours into apathy and resentment. "It's the middleness of everybody," says Larry Hirschhorn, with the Wharton Center for Applied Research. "Everybody feels in the middle; no one's on the top. There's a sense of people enmeshed in systems, so they can't control anything anymore."

Americans feel angry and powerless and it's affecting our work and attitude toward life. "More than ever before, Americans view school and work as an unpleasant interlude in their relaxation and entertainment, to be gotten out of the way with a minimum of effort," wrote Robert Eisenberger in *Blue Monday: The Loss of the Work Ethic in America.* "The decline of the work ethic has produced a majority culture of affluent Americans who will not work hard to maintain their comfortable standard of living, and a minority culture of poor Americans who will not persevere to overcome their impoverishment."

The decline of the work ethic is revealed in government statistics — it now takes more than three years to make the same productivity gains we used to achieve every year before 1973 — as well as everyday encounters with countrymen from all walks of life who feel they should be generously compensated even when they are lazy and stupid and their work is sloppy and careless.

A year or so ago, I called a painting contractor because the previous owner of our house had painted over wallpaper in several rooms. That wallpaper was peeling at the edges and had to be removed before new paint could be applied.

The contractor promised me it would be a cinch. I accepted his estimate, signed the contract, and he arrived with his crew. They were burly guys in denim jeans and vests, with long greasy hair, earrings, gap-toothed smiles, and lurid tattoos. Where, I wondered, had they parked their Harleys?

First they scraped off the old wallpaper — apparently with jackhammers. When I got home later that day, the walls of most of the rooms resembled the meteor-pocked surface of the moon. I called the contractor and complained. He assured me all the gouges and holes would be filled with plaster carefully and thoroughly. The next day, I found that a prime coat had been applied, even though most of the walls were still rough and scarred. I called the contractor again. Not to worry, he said. More filling would be done. On the third day, I was pleased at how nice the interior of the house looked — from a distance. Up close, and under light, the walls still looked like the Grand Canyon. I called the contractor.

"We did the best we could," he said. "What did you expect?"

"A professional job," I said.

I fired him and hired a new contractor. He was a glib, effusive man, who, as he toured the house, commiserated with me about the lousy work done by his predecessor. His men, he promised, would do a much better job.

As it turned out, his men were *worse.* Not only did they carve up the walls and fail to patch them, but they also dripped and spilled paint and missed several large spots. When I showed the painter a section about a foot square that his men had failed to paint in a bathroom, he looked at me as if I were crazy and neurotic.

"Hang a picture there," he said blithely. "No one will notice. Live your life!"

I went to see my grandfather on a hot summer day and was astonished that his air-conditioned house felt like a furnace. The central air conditioning system wasn't working, he told me, and he'd just paid a serviceman $125 to check it out and put it in tiptop condition. I went down to the basement to see whether anything was obviously wrong. The blower that's supposed to push cool air through the house wasn't working. The reason? The belt running from the motor to the blower was frayed and charred because some nitwit posing as an air-conditioning mechanic had installed it incorrectly. And the bearings on the blower shaft were so dry that I could barely turn it; they hadn't been lubricated in ages.

I drenched all the bearings with oil, replaced the drive belt, and tightened it to the proper tension. But when I switched the system on, I discovered something more dangerous: the insulation on the wires was worn and the wires were touching each other, which caused an immediate short as soon as I turned on the power.

The next day, I repaired the system myself in about an hour. I was proud, and my grandfather was grateful, but both of us couldn't help wondering what service — if any — the "serviceman" had given for his $125.

Recently, I called the U.S. Census Bureau for some information. What I got was one of those recorded Touchtone directory messages: "If you'd like information about population statistics, please press 1. If you'd like information about publications, please press 2. If you'd like to talk to a real live human being, please press 3. If you'd like to be put on hold for an hour, please press 4 . . ."

Forging ahead, I pressed what I thought was the appropriate button and after several minutes got yet another recorded voice: "Your call cannot be completed at this time; please try again later." I waited a half an hour and did so. No luck. As the day progressed, I called again, and again, and again. I tried different buttons, hoping to make contact with a live voice, but that didn't work, either.

The following day, I tried yet again. After two more attempts, I reached a human being, who managed to sound harried, bored, and ignorant all at once. When I asked her for information about the U.S. standard of living, she acted as if she'd never before heard the term or I was speaking a foreign tongue. She switched me to someone else, who gave me the name of another person to call. It took me a whole day to reach her, and she then told me she'd look into it and get back to me. Of course she never did. Several days later, when I asked for her by name, I was told she was on vacation. No one knew anything about my query or could help me. By now I knew that these people had a far different conception of their job from what I'd assumed. They weren't there to ferret out and dispense information; their job was to see how quickly and rudely they could deflect requests.

In the end, I still hadn't obtained the information I wanted. What if I'd been working on deadline and needed it immediately, I wondered. Also, how much were these helpful public servants making? And how much were we taxpayers wasting to support such worthless drones?

Right now, I have a blocked ear. It has been sealed shut for more than a month because of an unyielding cold and sinus infection. A couple weeks ago, I called the appropriate department at the Hospital of the University of Pennsylvania, Philadelphia's most prestigious hospital. The earliest appointment I could get to see a doctor was in a week; I took it. I showed up at the designated time but waited nearly two hours before a young man with an impatient, self-important manner quickly inspected my ear and told me I had an inner-ear infection. Nothing could be done, he said, except to wait until the fluids drained out naturally. For this brilliant revelation and helpful advice, he charged me $80.

After a week without relief, I telephoned the doctor's office and asked to speak to him. I wanted to find out whether I could do anything to hasten the healing process. The doctor didn't call that day. Nor the next. Nor the next. I continued calling. I telephoned a half-dozen times, leaving increasingly desperate messages with the doctor's secretary. A week later, my ear is still blocked, and the good doctor still hasn't returned any of my calls.

Are my expectations too high? Am I just a whining perfectionist? Sometimes I wonder. But then I hear similar tales of incompetence from friends and colleagues, people discouraged because it's nearly impossible to find anyone who really wants to work. Those who *say* they want to work too often do a lousy job.

It's no accident that a thriving industry has sprung up recently catering to do-it-yourselfers. People are patronizing home centers not just to save money but because they are fed up with tradesmen — carpenters, plumbers, electricians, painters, gardeners — who almost always do crummy work and let them down. The axiom "If you want something done right, do it yourself" has become the credo of many Americans who regard self-reliance not as a philosophical option but as a matter of survival.

America's work ethic is ailing not only among those who toil in blue collars, of course. People are afraid of hospitals because of the possibility that some negligent surgeon will take out the wrong organ, or some shiftless nurse will administer the wrong drug. A physician at a major teaching hospital complains, "Many patients don't know what's wrong with them, why tests are being ordered, why they're taking different medications, or what their doctor's thoughts are, because many physicians don't bother to talk to them. You go to get a mammogram — which can be very scary and emotional — you go through the hassle of waiting in the radiology suite and going through the test, and then it may take weeks before you find out the results, if you find out at all. Doctors and hospitals are generating enormous amounts of data that don't get processed half the time. It's as if you never had the test, because reports don't get back, or they get lost, or they go to the wrong place. Important information is never communicated."

Supreme Court Justice Anthony Kennedy says too many of today's lawyers show up in court unprepared. "We see shoddy practice in every court in the country, including the Supreme Court," he says. "We are sometimes very disappointed in the quality of oral arguments." Says a partner at a Philadelphia law firm: "There's a general sense that pride in craft is going out of the business, that we're churning out paper — churning out mediocre paper. We bitch and moan that we're no longer a profession, but we've done it to ourselves, because we don't act like a profession. We're consumed with minutiae, we're macho for the sake of being macho, we're obsessed with making money."

In my own profession, too many reporters gather information recklessly, don't bother to check facts, operate on unconfirmed assumptions, and write misleading and superficial stories because they simply don't take the time and make the effort to think. Confronted with factual errors, some shrug their shoulders and smirk. *Hey, don't be so anal. Everybody makes mistakes. It's only a newspaper. What's the big deal?*

Somehow hard work has become both unhip and positively un-American. *"Workin' hard?" "Hell no, I'm hardly workin'."* The new American Dream is winning the lottery — riches without effort, reward without talent, gain without pain. "Americans are addicted to the consumption of energy, to profligate plastics and convenience power in all its fuming, humming expressions — cars, motorboats, air conditioners, home appliances," Lance Morrow wrote in *Time.* "They are addicted to credit and debt, to mobility, to high speed. The American addictions tend to have this in common: a hope of painlessness . . . The idea of the nation's Manifest Destiny, of its ascendant virtue and inevitable success, was driven in the past by the professed ethic of hard work and sacrifice. But somewhere, the hardworking part of the formula got lost. Did the American Dream all along mean nothing more than the quest for painlessness?"

Television spills its electronic cornucopia into our living rooms, stirring greed and envy, sapping initiative and imagination, seducing and enervating with its incessant message of instant gratification and sensual pleasure. As our nation — self-deluding, improvident, and allergic to reality — hurtles toward the millennium on cruise control, our latest, hottest cultural hero is Bart Simpson, that flippant cartoon character who's inspired millions of American youngsters to buy T-shirts proclaiming UNDERACHIEVER — AND PROUD OF IT. "Television used to demean working-class jobs; now any kind of work is demeaning," says Eisenberger. "When does Bill Cosby go into work? Work and competence are not part of the world television presents."

Middle-class parents have grandiose dreams for their children, but too often spoil them so royally that they reach adulthood without the tools to achieve those dreams. Most Americans don't want their children to grow up to be cowboys — or carpenters, plumbers, auto mechanics, or roofers, either. They hope their kids will go to college, and work in an office — and make big bucks.

"Today's society places excessive pressure on students to get a college degree," says Garry O'Rourke, a houseparent at Girard College, a private school in Philadelphia. "Students and parents view it as an almost automatic key to a satisfying and rewarding career, and secondary schools love to boast a high percentage of graduates who continue to college. I am concerned that our work force of tradespeople is going to dwindle both in absolute numbers and level of competence. No more eloquent summation of this issue can be had than that of the writer John Gardner: 'The society which scorns excellence in plumbing because it is a humble activity and tolerates shoddiness in philosophy because it is an exalted activity will have neither good plumbing nor good philosophy. Neither its pipes nor its theories will hold water.' "

In Japan, a person can take pride in being a superb janitor; the Japanese are taught that every job is important, because every worker is rendering a service to society. The only thing shameful is to do your work poorly. In the United States, by contrast, if you're a janitor or housekeeper, you're a loser, whether you do your job carefully or sloppily. In fact, if you do it carefully, you're considered a sucker.

America's schools and colleges have already taken a beating in this book, but disrespect for work often does begin in the classroom, the very place where good work habits should be formed. The Princeton University economist Uwe E. Reinhardt says, "I've watched the homework of my children, and I'm appalled at the junk they're allowed to hand in. Eighty percent of the teachers have zero work standards; most don't check homework at all. American teachers accept work for which in Europe a child would literally get slapped."

In high school and college, the game is to do just enough, and only enough, to get by. It is a game that often involves cheating (surveys reveal that anywhere from 40 percent to 90 percent of students today cheat on tests and papers) by dunces who are trying to avoid flunking out and by honor students who view education primarily as a way of getting the grades they need, and the degrees and honors they need, and the transcripts and credentials they need, to land a job that starts at $60,000 a year. Many students want to succeed without making any effort to comprehend. Their attitude: some subordinate will do the detail and analysis work for them, so they don't have to understand.

"American students are shying away from difficult courses in areas like engineering, mathematics, and chemistry," Eisenberger says. "The reason is that these courses haven't been watered down to the same extent as other courses. Students want to get their degrees and make a lot of money without having to work hard. That's why in America, at both the undergraduate and graduate levels, the difficult courses are being filled by foreign students. We are importing not only cheap labor but also the brains of everybody from around the world. In fact, the Defense Department is worried that soon we won't have enough Americans to work on top-secret projects, that our supposedly secret research labs will be filled with foreigners who will return one day to their countries, taking their expertise with them and perhaps American military and scientific secrets as well."

Inspired by Michael Milken and other get-rich-quick sleazeballs who prospered during the Decade of the Deal, college students have been flocking to business schools rather than enrolling in engineering programs that teach them to apply scientific, mathematical, and technological principles toward solving problems. In 1986, nearly half the senior class at Yale applied for jobs at First Boston Corporation, a Wall Street investment firm that bankrolled many of the corporate raiders of the 1980s. The goal of many elite students was to snare a high-powered, money-moving job right out of college, to hustle hard and make a million dollars before they turned thirty, and to bail out so that they could spend the rest of their lives not working.

From a peak of about seventy-seven thousand in the mid-1980s, the number of engineering graduates has declined steadily. Equally alarming, the number of college freshmen enrolled in engineering programs has eroded 20 percent since 1983. One reason: the work's too tough. M. Richard Rose, president of the Rochester Institute of Technology in New York, laments, "Many college kids are products of affluence; they haven't had to mow lawns or milk the cows. The work may have been a pain, but it did teach you daily discipline."

While Harvard and other elite law schools are teaching America's academic cream how to generate paper and clog the courts, our nation's engineering schools are teaching thousands of eager students from *other* countries how to conceive and improve products, streamline manufacturing, create new jobs and new industries and new wealth, and elevate the standard of living. Today, over half the new recipients of doctoral degrees in engineering and more than a third of the engineering faculty members in the United States were born in other countries. In 1988, foreign inventors received half of all U.S. patents. "We're becoming a litigious, not a design, society," says Rose.

The consequences are indisputable: without sufficient technical expertise, the United States can't compete. In international trade, we will fall farther and farther behind such formidable rivals as Germany and Japan. (Though its population is only half as big as ours, Japan graduates twice as many engineers as we do.) Nor will we be able to fix all the roads, bridges, and water and sewer systems that compose our nation's crumbling infrastructure. Betty Vetter, executive director of the Commission on Professionals in Science and Technology, a nonprofit group in Washington, says, "The number of civil engineers alone that will be needed to rebuild the nation's cities will probably be ten times as many as we could hope to have." Our disdain for manufacturing — and for the engineering proficiency that is vital to it — may lead to the day when our main industry is selling franchised hamburgers, when we're paying off our foreign debt by doing the rest of the world's laundry.

None of this seems to faze the yuppie lawyers, bankers, and stockbrokers in their official Gordon Gekko pinstripes, power ties, and red suspenders. After all, until recently, they were still reaping obscene rewards for "engineering" transactions. They were still earning six-figure salaries, and more, for merging and acquiring, leveraging and restructuring, consolidating and diversifying. And for their quick wit and canniness, their keen eye for fees and margins and profits, and their frantic fax-ruled seventy-hour weeks, these "Big Swinging Dicks" of corporate law and high finance were enjoying the emoluments they believed they deserved: the spacious co-op overlooking Central Park, the weekend retreat in the Berk-shires, the charcoal-gray Saab Turbo convertible with the Clarion AM-FM stereo cassette system with electronically tuned reception. What did it matter if their "work" had no social value or larger purpose; if they paid no heed to long-range consequences (debt-crippled companies, forced wage concessions, slashed jobs, bankruptcies, ruined lives) and the future, except, of course, their own future and that golden day when, having amassed sufficient millions to survive in pluto-cratic style, they could flee the vipers' pit and retire to Nan-tucket, ideally before their fortieth birthday — or before the collapse of the house of cards they had worked so diligently to erect?

The economist Reinhardt wrote, in a recent issue of the *Princeton Alumni Weekly*, "In our complex, modern world . . . large private fortunes can easily be extracted by clever folks from less-clever folks through imaginative zero-sum or negative-sum games. As I often tell my students . . . 'You may become engineers, physicians, or product entrepreneurs who earn your income as a reward for contributing to the welfare and prosperity of society as a whole . . . On the other hand, you may join the ever-growing corps of income redistribu-tors — tax experts, legal experts, regulatory experts, financial wizards, lobbyists, legislators, and so on — who use so much of their time and intellect not to create net social value added, but merely to redistribute toward themselves and their clients claims to the useful production of others.' "

My beloved Irish grandfather is a powerful talker, and one of the things he talks about a lot these days is America's declin-ing work ethic.

If you spent an hour listening to him over a meal of corned beef and cabbage, I'll bet you'd hear him marvel about how the Empire State Building was built in only fifteen months, and how, in 1926, a Chicago mason laid six hundred blocks a day; today, it takes two masons that long to lay one hundred blocks.

Certainly he'd also tell you about the nation's Centennial Exposition, which was held in Philadelphia's Fairmount Park in 1876. It opened exactly one year after boosters broke ground for the fair, and during those twelve months, a phenomenal group of energetic men, working without today's bulldozers, earthmovers, cranes, and other power equipment, cleared 240 acres of parkland, built 250 structures, including several magnificent stone-and-cast-iron buildings that still stand, paved more than seven miles of road, and transported and installed more than fifty thousand cases of exhibits, weighing in all more than twenty thousand tons.

My grandfather is well aware that working conditions were horrible in those days, that many laborers were little better than slaves, toiling sixty to eighty hours a week, suffering from disease, dying young in accidents on the job. Nevertheless, he can't help comparing that achievement with the progress made on Philadelphia's half-billion-dollar convention center — a project that's been on the drawing board for nearly a decade and, because of squabbles over money and politics, is little more than a hole in the ground. Optimists say the center will be finished and ready for business in three years. A more realistic estimate is four years — and probably longer.

I consider my grandfather an expert on work; he's always been a hard worker himself and he's had a long, long time to observe, study, and think about work. He was born in 1897 and has seen a huge chunk of American history. When he was a boy, the Sheepshead Bay area of Brooklyn, where he grew up, was all farmland. One Sunday when he was fourteen, he ran over to the local racetrack and helped launch the biplane that made the first flight across the continent.

Like many boys of his time, he was forced to quit high school and get a job so that he could contribute to the family. He did so without complaint, deferring, forever, a fond dream of attending Cornell. He began as an office boy for a specialty-steel company in Manhattan, then worked his way up to salesman. In the early 1920s, he was assigned to open an office in Philadelphia, and in 1929 he began his own business, representing manufacturers of machine tools. He couldn't have chosen a worse time; the Depression nearly wiped him out. One year, he earned only $600. With a wife and four children, he had to scramble for whatever cash he could. All week long, traveling by trolley and train, he visited machine shops and manufacturing plants, hoping to scare up enough orders for spare parts to survive. In the evenings, he worked as a bill collector. For a time, he even tried writing screenplays at a picnic table in Fairmount Park. Warner Brothers liked one enough to "borrow" most of the plot for a movie starring Joe E. Brown; my grandfather received not a penny.

By the time World War II broke out, my grandfather's business was prospering. His hard work paid off, and the economy recovered. He supplied huge machine tools — presses and brakes and shears — to companies like Bethlehem Steel and Budd, as well as to many other manufacturing firms that then constituted the economic backbone of Philadelphia.

Today, many of those companies — Baldwin Locomotive, Henry Disston & Sons, Philco, and Westinghouse, to name a few — have either closed altogether or packed up and left Philadelphia. And today my grandfather just shakes his head in amazement and disbelief at what's left of the city's once-mighty manufacturing base.

"From the turn of the century until the end of World War II, Philadelphia was a center of heavy industry," he told me recently. "On the Delaware River, which was once known as 'the Clyde of America,' there were six large shipyards between Bristol, Pennsylvania, and Wilmington. North Philadelphia was famous for manufacturing. There were hundreds of factories and mills and machine shops and metal fabricators. Today, most of that has vanished.

"Now what we have are these so-called service industries. The new office buildings downtown are filled mostly with lawyers and investment advisers and business consultants. Who are they counseling? Who are they advising? Who are they consulting with? I don't understand how these industries are surviving.

"The basis of any economy is the production of goods; the basis of commerce is manufacturing. You take something out of the ground and you use your brains and tools and you make something out of it and try to sell it. But Americans today don't like to make things. Manufacturing is too grimy and unglamorous. They'd rather let Korea and Taiwan do it. Americans would rather shuffle papers than dirty their hands."

Bethlehem Steel — a company where my grandfather did so much business and spent so much time that he felt almost like an employee — was once a robust industrial colossus that built more than eleven hundred ships during World War II, erected the Golden Gate and George Washington bridges, New York's Waldorf-Astoria, Chicago's Merchandise Mart, Washington's National Gallery of Art, and scores of the nation's missile silos. Today it is on the ropes, an aged, feeble giant, shedding plants and employees to trim costs and survive.

My grandfather only laughs incredulously. "Forty years ago, if you'd questioned Bethlehem Steel's credit, people would have thought you were joking or out of your mind. No one would have imagined, in their wildest dreams, that the day would come when Bethlehem Steel would contemplate filing under Chapter Eleven or that the company would someday be so strapped that they'd have to sell their headquarters building."

Looking back, it's easy to see how Bethlehem Steel blew it, my grandfather says. "In a nutshell, the whole company — both management and labor — lost the work ethic. In the lush days, when Bethlehem was the number two steelmaker in the United States and the profits were rolling in, the company's top executives were handing themselves unconscionable bonuses instead of pouring that money into new technology and equipment. They were so convinced that Bethlehem was omnipotent and invincible that they paid more attention to their golf handicaps at the Saucon Valley Country Club than to innovations in the industry and the threat of foreign competition. For a while, it seemed every time they produced a ton of steel, Bethlehem created a new vice president.

"When it came to dealing with labor, Bethlehem just rolled over and yielded to union demands so they could avoid unpleasant strikes. The result was outrageous featherbedding, and wage rates that went up to the point that by the early eighties steelworkers were making more than $26 an hour — about twice as much as the average manufacturing worker. This was completely unrealistic, and there was no way it could continue.

"Then Bethlehem Steel woke up one day to find that they were behind the parade, that they were outclassed, that the Koreans had the most advanced, up-to-date steel-manufacturing plant in the world. By then, Bethlehem had to scramble just to avoid collapsing. They started shutting down plants and laying off workers. They closed down the Lackawanna plant. They reduced operations at Johnstown. They closed down the Lebanon fastener plant. They cut back at Steelton. They got out of the shipbuilding business altogether.

"Now it's almost painful for me to go to Bethlehem. The

plant that was so bustling when I was making calls there is like a ghost town today. It's really a modern industrial tragedy — a sad, sorry saga of laziness, complacency, and incompetence."

The woes of Bethlehem Steel are not unique. In many ways, the story of its rise and fall is an allegory of what has happened to American industry. It is the story of our steel industry, our automobile industry, our electronics industry, our shipping industry. And if we don't wake up, it may soon become the story of such twenty-first-century industries as semiconductors, supercomputers, industrial robots, superconductivity, and biotechnology.

Who's at fault? Much of the blame falls squarely on the shoulders of America's managers. They have failed to manufacture competitive products efficiently and carefully because they've failed to train workers for more sophisticated jobs or to manage employees in a way that encourages competence, dedication, and hard work. The Japanese are committed to training and preparing their workers as a matter of national policy. The result is a high-performance, front-line labor force that can think and act autonomously. Although the United States invests heavily in college students, it shortchanges young people who look for work right after high school. Our nation spends more than twice as much educating college kids as it does training non-college-bound youth, the General Accounting Office says.

"Less than 1 percent of our businesses are spending 95 percent of the training money," former Labor Secretary Brock told *Time*. "Most are doing very little, and the ones that are doing very much are using their funds to train management. There is almost nothing in most companies for the great majority of workers, but the work place is changing underneath their feet. The average young person coming out of high school today will have at least four to six jobs in his working life, two to three different careers. If workers are given continuing training and education by firms they work for, that is not going to be a problem. If they are not, we are going to leave 15 percent to 30 percent off to the side of the road every year."

The United Kingdom, Sweden, Japan, and West Germany each spends proportionately more than the United States in helping those with a manual, technical, or vocational bent achieve their full potential — and it shows. "The shoddiness of American workmanship is a direct reflection of the absence of an apprenticeship system," says Princeton's Reinhardt, who received his training in Germany. Except in medicine and some trade unions, America lacks such a system, and we're worse off because of it.

"The predominant objective of an apprenticeship system is to create a proper attitude toward work," Reinhardt says. "When I was a young man, I worked as an apprentice in an export-forwarding department. I had a boss standing behind me as I entered numbers into the ledger. If he saw me do it sloppily, he scolded me. If I did it again, he hit me. I learned quickly to do it right. My friends who were becoming engineers spent the first half of the year filing metal to fit through a triangular hole. What better way to teach the importance of precision? And that's how it's done all through Europe.

"To learn the trade next to a master who . . . guides you and helps you avoid mistakes creates a certain pride in your work. In the European apprenticeship system, more than teaching is passed on; a certain ethos is passed on, too. You learn from your master certain skills and certain character traits — integrity, dignity, and a sense that, no matter what you do, if you do it well, you are somebody."

Workers who are "somebodies" usually have a healthy work ethic. In other words, workers who have skills, and are proud of their skills, and are appreciated enough to be given the time, tools, and supplies to exercise their skills properly, will usually work hard. But this truism is beyond the comprehension of many American managers, whose approach to organizing production and boosting productivity hasn't changed since the days of Frederick Winslow Taylor: dumb down the jobs and speed up the work. At many companies, numbers crunchers and bottom-line-oriented micromanagers are unwittingly undermining the work ethic by forcing their employees to work harder and faster — to produce better results, with fewer resources, in less time. Many workers are actually *punished* for behavior that, in another context, would be viewed as evidence of conscientiousness and competence. Some service representatives, for example, are policed electronically and penalized for spending too much time with customers. Of the seventeen million office workers who operate video display terminals, an estimated 20 to 40 percent are monitored by computers. At Pacific Southwest Airlines in San Diego, reservation agents are expected to average 109 seconds per call and 11 seconds between calls, during which they're required to complete paperwork. The emphasis on speed reduces the quality of service. In some cases, looking up answers to any but the simplest questions can cost operators and service representatives their jobs. Consequently, many dispense incorrect or incomplete information, or they respond in such a testy, abrupt manner that they offend and alienate customers.

Often orchestrated by MBA types who believe all management problems can be reduced to a mathematical equation, speed-ups have caused many clerical workers to cut corners. Rushed and frustrated, they ignore consumer questions about bills and throw away letters unanswered. In 1985, overwhelmed workers at an IRS processing center in Philadelphia lost, destroyed, or discarded thousands of tax returns.

To meet work quotas, exhausted employees and managers in the mailroom failed to open many letters and documents, and some stressed-out workers tossed unprocessed tax returns and tax payments totaling hundreds of thousands of dollars into a trash barrel bound for an incinerator. At the IRS's Los Angeles center, an overworked clerk was indicted because he'd kept forty bags of mail at his home — including more than $800,000 in taxpayer checks — in order to make himself appear more efficient.

At many companies, the relationship between management and labor today is more than adversarial; it's downright acrimonious. Several of the firms that loaded up debt in the 1980s and then began sinking have tried to bail themselves out by throwing their workers overboard first. That happened at Greyhound and at Eastern Airlines, two once-thriving American businesses that were felled by the rapacity of leveraged-buyout kings and corporate raiders. For instance, when Texas Air acquired Eastern, the takeover burdened the airline with a crushing $2.5 billion debt. Eastern was losing $1 million a day, mostly because of inflated interest payments. To stop the hemorrhaging, Texas Air demanded that Eastern's unionized machinists and baggage handlers accept a wage cut of 40 percent! Needless to say, the workers hit the bricks. The labor strife compounded Eastern's hardships and the company filed for bankruptcy. Nearly two years later, in January 1991, the sixty-two-year-old airline made famous under the direction of the World War I flying ace Eddie Rickenbacker shut down and began liquidating its assets.

Emboldened by the antiunion spirit of the Reagan years, many corporations have gotten macho. While businessmen in Europe and Asia are making extraordinary progress by treating workers with respect, sharing decision making and creating a sense of mutual trust and joint enterprise, many of America's executives — flinty-eyed, thin-lipped, stingy, and suspicious — are bullying workers, crusading to bust unions, threatening to move jobs down south or overseas, refusing to bargain in good faith, provoking nasty internecine labor wars, such as the strike by the United Mine Workers against Pittston Coal and newspaper unions against the *New York Daily News*.

The unions are hardly blameless. In fact, many are getting their just deserts. For too long, the American economy has been hamstrung by labor unions that seemed to be less interested in labor than in destroying what's left of the American work ethic. On some construction jobs, union electricians and mechanics are paid a full day's wages for simply turning a machine on at the beginning of a shift and turning it off at the end. Outrageous union work rules were a major cause of Bethlehem Steel's demise. "A multiplicity of high-paid craftsmen continued to feed on routine jobs that a single worker could perform cheaper and faster," reported John Strohmeyer in *Crisis in Bethlehem: Big Steel's Struggle to Survive.* "With the industry in peril, an electrician, a motor repairman and usually a laborer still had to be called in on a simple motor repair job, even if only a fan belt adjustment was needed."

At the *Philadelphia Inquirer*, the Newspaper Guild represents most of the paper's editorial employees (including me). Thanks to the union, several hacks, prima donnas, misfits, and mental cases who are laughably inept and who rarely do a lick of work are guaranteed a paycheck until the day they retire or die. The *Inquirer*'s lunatic asylum includes a few feeble-minded editors who can be depended on to screw up every time, no matter what the task, as well as a contingent of sulky reporters and writers so unproductive they seem to operate on a monthly cycle, contributing a slim story once every four weeks or so, if that. Interestingly, some of these same people are among the most vociferous when it comes to trashing management and pressing union demands for higher pay and more benefits.

For a couple of years after college, I worked for an independent telephone workers' union as editor of its monthly magazine. Ostensibly the union's mission was to safeguard and enhance the economic welfare of its members, and it preached a gospel of worker pride and dignity. But the union's real business was promoting a sense of grievance, victimization, and entitlement.

The union leaders justified their existence and kept their jobs by constantly reminding workers how they'd been used and abused by management, how they deserved better treatment and a bigger slice of the pie. Workers were never to blame; it was always the company's fault. The workers had rights; the company had responsibilities. The union wanted it both ways: Pride and Victimhood simultaneously. But you can't be proud and a victim too. Victims don't do; they have things done *to* them. They are essentially passive and powerless. And a person without power is a person without dignity. And a person without dignity has nothing to be proud about.

Grievance, victimization, and entitlement are not confined to organized labor; they are also at the heart of affirmative action, a well-intentioned experiment in social engineering that has further eroded America's work ethic. The idea behind it — to include the excluded, to create more job opportunities for women and blacks, to make up for past discrimination, to force companies and institutions to put their money where their mouths are — is laudable. But in practice, affirmative action often does more harm than good, demoralizing not only white males (the group usually blamed for all the world's woes) but also blacks and women (affirmative action's supposed beneficiaries).

As originally conceived, affirmative action "meant casting the net wide to admit people or hire people who would otherwise be missed," says Princeton sociology professor Howard F. Taylor. That's an idea I did, and do, support wholeheartedly. Furthermore, I agree — and am delighted — that affirmative action has given many capable, talented people who formerly might have been overlooked or deliberately rejected for racial and sexual reasons a chance to show their stuff, to everybody's benefit.

In recent years, however, I've become disillusioned with affirmative action, and especially the quotas — often disguised as "goals" — employed to achieve it. It's become, like abortion, an emotionally charged ideological litmus test, a shibboleth of such sanctity that even to question it is to run the risk of being written off as a racist. Once a lever for enhancing opportunity, affirmative action has become a cudgel for artificially accelerating positive social changes set in motion by the civil rights movement. Those changes, rational and evolutionary, are now being hastened and enforced with a totalitarian fervor that borders on the reckless and revolutionary. To be sure, affirmative action has put teeth in efforts to increase the participation of blacks and women to levels more representative of the general population (which is good). On the other hand, in the name of affirmative action, advocates of social progress have frequently fudged or ignored the troubling issue of qualifications and distorted, diluted, or discarded standards of excellence (which is very bad).

On a more basic philosophical level, the fatal flaw of affirmative action is that it tries to fix a wrong with a wrong. It is not, primarily, about merit (a dirty, racially loaded word in some quarters today). Nor is it about equal opportunity. It's about creating "diversity" by giving preference to people of a certain race, sex, or ethnic background. To compensate for past racism, it sanctions a racist remedy.

Affirmative action is wrong for the same reason that a

company that proclaims itself "an affirmative action, equal opportunity employer" is contradicting itself. Affirmative action is "equal opportunity, but . . ." — some are more equal than others. By granting an unfair advantage to people of a certain race or sex, no matter how much that advantage may seem historically justified, affirmative action violates *equal* opportunity. You can't have it both ways. "You cannot claim both full equality and special dispensation," says *Washington Post* columnist William Raspberry.

In addition, by emphasizing our differences, by encouraging a poisonous racial, sexual, and ethnic self-consciousness, affirmative action divides rather than unites. In seeking to redress past injustices and resentments, it creates new injustices and resentments. It has the potential to rend organizations into hostile factions animated by grudge and grievance. It classifies and stereotypes people by race and gender, and fails to acknowledge how unique we all are as individuals.

Recently, I attended a seminar at the *Philadelphia Inquirer* during which a bright, articulate black woman explained the company's "pluralism" program. Responding to questions, she said, in effect, that white males had had their day and that it was time for them to step aside and make room for women and people of color. As she said this, I looked around the room to see how others were reacting. No one batted an eye or said a thing. Several people nodded assent. I was astonished. Here, at a newspaper that prides itself on being a bastion of liberalism, no one seemed the least bit upset that someone's race or sex might take precedence over a person's ability as a reporter, writer, editor, or photographer.

Clearly, ours is a racist, sexist society, and special efforts must be made to reach out to blacks and women. Certainly, there are circumstances when being black or female or of a certain ethnic heritage is, in itself, a qualification that should carry weight — for example, at a newspaper that is conscientiously trying to cover a city with a sizable black or Hispanic population. The problem, though, is that under the banner of affirmative action many unprepared, unqualified people have been brought aboard and prematurely pushed along. Some have risen to the occasion, succeeding beyond the most optimistic predictions through pluck, determination, and sheer native ability. But others have failed spectacularly. Those failures — often ignored or rationalized away — have been embarrassing, humiliating affairs, harming the organizations where those people worked and disillusioning well-wishers and supporters. Even worse, they've reinforced negative stereotypes, stigmatized those who are truly able and deserving, and embittered those who've been passed over for reasons they can't do a thing about — such as lacking the right skin pigmentation or sex organs. Most tragically, such failures have scarred the very men and women affirmative action was designed to help. Their self-esteem in tatters, they may become alienated and hostile, blaming their shortcomings on the institutions that offered them the chance to succeed in the first place.

"I believe affirmative action is problematic in our society because we have demanded that it create parity between the races rather then insure equal opportunity," argues Shelby Steele, an English professor at San Jose State University in California, in a *New York Times Magazine* article which was drawn from his book *The Content of Our Character: A New Vision of Race in America*. Affirmative action implies white superiority and black inferiority, Steele says, thereby reinforcing a debilitating racial doubt. It also "indirectly encourages blacks to exploit their own past victimization. Like implied inferiority, victimization is what justifies preference, so that to receive the benefits of preferential treatment one must, to some extent, become invested in the view of one's self as a victim. In this way, affirmative action nurtures a victim-focused identity in blacks and sends us the message that there is more power in our past suffering than in our present achievements."

Affirmative action is presumptuous and patronizing. It is, as Charles Krauthammer has observed, "a demeaning form of racial tutelage." It is based on the racist and sexist assumption that blacks and women can't compete, that without the social handicapping of preferential treatment or formal set-asides, blacks and women will almost always lose out to white males. What else can such preferences mean? When affirmative action is the policy, the accomplishments of all blacks and women are devalued. Those with high-profile jobs and fast-track careers are subject to suspicion: Did they get there on their own or were they jet-propelled by quotas?

More to the point, by discounting merit, however slightly, affirmative action damages the work ethic. The implication of affirmative action is that it isn't what you do or how well you do it that is important; it's whether you possess certain superficial attributes that enable companies to assuage their corporate guilt by meeting quotas, tacit or explicit. Affirmative action breeds cynicism, disaffection, arrogance, and indolence. It saps initiative and offers a ready rationale for infantile whiners, chronic malcontents, and those who feel they're owed more than they've earned. It encourages the belief in some that working hard and excelling are no longer worth it because working hard and excelling are no longer what matter most. And it fosters the attitude in others that they're special exceptions, exempt from normal standards and expectations, deserving of advancement on principle rather than performance.

Sure, examples abound of white male bozos, peabrains, and ne'er-do-wells who've gotten ahead because of the old boy network, or the old school tie, or social connections, inherited wealth, and who their parents were. But affirmative action, by institutionalizing privilege based on race and sex, mocks the notion of meritocracy in a formal, frontal way and engenders instead an invidious culture of entitlement.

Moreover, its basic premise — that all white males enjoy an edge because they are white and male — is simply no longer true. In fact, at many places the opposite is the case. For a talented, diligent woman or person of color, the opportunities today are dazzling. By contrast, to be a white male, more and more, is to have two strikes against you.

For the past two years, a white male friend of mine has been trying to land a newspaper job in New York City. An Ivy League graduate with plenty of journalistic seasoning, he is a first-rate reporter and writer with a special interest in urban issues. Several times he applied for jobs, aced the requisite interviews, but was told by prospective employers that his qualifications are superb and that they'd hire him in a second — if only he were a "minority" or, better yet, a "minority" woman. My friend is an unabashed liberal and a staunch believer in minority advancement and women's rights, but he can't help feeling frustrated and more than a little discouraged about being an innocent scapegoat for the inequities of the past.

In the final analysis, affirmative action is repugnant because it requires a hypocritical violation of principle. An organization that hires and promotes on the basis of race and sex can no longer claim that it does not discriminate on the basis of race and sex. It can no longer claim that it is an equal opportunity employer. It can no longer pretend to be a meritocracy. It is this inconsistency, I think, that makes even the most fervent supporters of racial and sexual equality feel uneasy, deep down inside, about affirmative action. It's also the reason such plans frequently run afoul of the law. For all the noble intentions and carefully crafted language, affirmative action is, at root, a violation of the very promise of America — the promise that here, as nowhere else in the world, people of every description can, through talent and hard work, transcend the conditions of their birth, become whatever they want, realize the most extravagant dreams.

In reality, that promise often has not been kept, of course. But the odds today are probably more favorable than ever before. And so the promise still beckons millions to our shores. Though their hopes and schemes may vary, they share the conviction that America's bounty is theirs for the working. "The most motivated Americans today are the immigrants — the Cubans, the Japanese, the Koreans," says Eisenberger. "It used to be that America would shape a stronger work ethic, teaching immigrants the idea of getting ahead by doing a good job. Now, the immigrants are coming here with stronger work values. But the longer they stay, and the longer they're exposed to American culture, the weaker those values become."

America must take affirmative action, all right — to shore up its ailing work ethic. Freud spoke the truth when he said that happiness is *liebe und arbeit* — love and work. Somewhere along the way, we got seduced by our sustained prosperity into believing that happiness is freedom from work, that the definition of bliss is infinite leisure. Besides the fact that most of us must work if we're going to eat, leisure has no meaning unless it's a respite from work. For work is what makes leisure special and precious. Work is what defines and empowers us. Work, no matter how humble, gives us a role, a part to play, in the universal drama of human survival. Work is our daily imitation of God's ordering the chaos of the cosmos, creating something from nothing. Work is proof of our competence and faith in ourselves — as individuals and as a nation. "Great civilizations

are born stoic and die epicurean," the historian Will Durant
once remarked. America's declining work ethic portends
something much more serious than a moribund economy. It
is symptomatic of a disease of the spirit, a distorted sense of
human satisfaction and what it takes to make life truly
worthwhile.

7 The Decline of Quality

An executive at a major construction company:
"The skins are coming off buildings more now because architects are not designing them properly. The architects are no longer designing the buildings; they're just designing the esthetics, and peeling off responsibility for high-risk details — such as connecting and hanging the building skins — on the contractors and subcontractors who often don't have the professional background to ensure that this work is structurally sound.

"It's all part of a risk-management game — played by lawyers and insurance companies and driven by competitive bidding and the profit motive — that's encouraged architects to provide what's known in the building business as 'lowest admissible quality.' This, in turn, has resulted in crummy, sometimes dangerous buildings, an avalanche of lawsuits for 'errors and omissions,' and a general decline in construction standards and industry pride . . .

"Many subcontractors are totally irresponsible. They don't show up on time. They don't do what they're supposed to do. They don't work. Their main motivation is money, to squeeze as much profit out of their bid as possible by getting the work done as fast as possible, by taking short cuts and cutting corners and using substandard materials — whatever they can get away with while the general contractor isn't watching.

"The unions don't recognize quality. They believe in

the brotherhood concept: everybody's equal. They don't reward the excellent mechanics and punish the bums. These guys have had it so good for so long that they don't know what reality is anymore . . . It's no different from American politics. It's self-serving through and through, all down the line. The first priority is me, the second is the union, the third is the work I produce — sometimes.

"People don't care the way they used to. They don't have pride in the product. You see it in management as well as in the trades. Yuppies come with minimum experience and expect maximum responsibility and income. They work as an assistant superintendent on one building and think they're ready to be a superintendent on the next. They're hard-working, but in a ruthless way.

"Ambition has replaced quality, dedication, and loyalty."

A TTENTION, K mart shoppers!
We waste our money on cheaply made junk and plastic schlock. We live in cardboard houses filled with particle-board furniture in highway-interchange communities dominated by fast-food restaurants and gaudy shopping malls, those cathedrals of consumerism where we run up our Visa bills and run down our souls.

We drown our better instincts in a sea of "popular culture" (a rarely acknowledged oxymoron). In art, in music, in literature, the trashy and transient are celebrated. *Have you read Vanna's autobiography?* Television has become the window into our collective psyche. And what does one see when one peers into the tube? *Entertainment Tonight.* We confuse democracy with the apotheosis of mass taste, our national vitality with fierce vulgarity. Tabloids tout our cultural icons: Hulk Hogan, glowering muscle-bound menace, Roseanne

Barr, screeching "The Star-Spangled Banner," saluting the home of the knave, the land of the slob.

Little wonder, then, that incompetence is rampant in America, because incompetence is both the cause and result of the decline of quality. Incompetents do not produce quality; when quality is not expected, incompetents thrive. It's the dynamic of terminal philistinism.

Quality, admittedly, is subjective: one person's idea of quality may be another's idea of schlock, and vice versa. On the other hand, quality is one of those words, like *class*, which people generally agree about. Grace Kelly had class; Madonna doesn't. Quality is difficult to define, easy to recognize; we know it when we see it. In the realm of goods and services, quality is less ambiguous. Quality is strong and solid. It is fine and beautiful. Quality is reliable and durable, attentive and responsive. It is inspiring and enriching. In a word, quality is superior.

Quality is both a state and a state of mind, the condition sought by those who strive to excel, to reach perfection, to transcend the flimsy and shoddy, the crude and gross, the trivial and ephemeral, the disgusting and demeaning. Ultimately, quality is about improving human nature and overcoming human fallibility and, with great pluck and style and a godlike nod to eternity, defying mortality itself by struggling, no matter how humble the endeavor, to make the best of it, to contribute something valuable and lasting.

America has always had an uneasy relationship with quality. Business seeks to create the widest possible market for its goods and services, playing to the lowest common denominator, maximizing profits by reducing costs and, frequently, compromising quality. As consumers, however, we hope for quality, and are dismayed when we don't receive it. Quality is also a component of superiority, and being on top, being number one (or at least feeling that we are) has been, until recently, a salient American ambition.

Today, the word *quality* is on everybody's lips. Corporate America has made quality a slogan, a buzzword, almost a fetish. It is emblazoned in every advertisement, proclaimed in every TV commercial. America's automakers don't seem to be selling cars today; they're marketing the image of quality. Businessmen rush to embrace the quality principles of W. Edwards Deming, the American statistician and quality-control guru who revitalized Japanese industry after the war. Many companies now have "quality circles" and "quality resource groups" and "quality improvement programs."

We are greatly indebted to Japan for all this. Our one-time protégé has been reminding us what quality is and showing us how it can and should be achieved. We also owe thanks to much of the rest of the world for letting us know that our products are not up to snuff by refusing to buy them. Which is one reason for our ghastly foreign trade imbalances.

Happily, all the talk and attention to quality lately have begun to make a difference. Numerous American corporations have invested billions of dollars in the most advanced plant and equipment. General Motors, for instance, spent eight years and $3.5 billion to develop a new car called Saturn, which it hopes will prove that the United States can manufacture small cars as high in quality as those built by the Japanese. Many other companies — Black and Decker, Motorola, and Xerox among them — are making a sincere effort to provide better products and better service, to convert wary consumers who long ago decided that anything made in America is, ipso facto, suspect and probably sure to break or fail.

Enlightened managers have started to re-examine how they organize production and manage people. They've begun treating workers like "human resources" rather than expendable cogs in an industrial machine. They now relegate mindless, repetitious, mechanized tasks to more efficient robots. And they emphasize quality; they take the time to develop and test a product until it defies improvement, and then they encourage employees, who are glad of the opportunity to take pride in their work, to make it so carefully and flawlessly that the customer is unfailingly satisfied.

Unfortunately, however, such companies are still the exception. Most American corporations still cling to their old ways. Managers may boast of their commitment to quality and make high-sounding speeches about vision and long-range plans and investing in the future, but most are slaves to the Wall Street analysts. When all is said and done, they lust for higher quarterly dividends — the leading addiction of America's executive class — which are often achieved by cutting costs, cutting workers, and cutting the very thing they profess to strive for — quality.

In Marysville, Ohio, American workers build Accords whose quality rivals or exceeds the same cars built in Japanese plants. "All of this pessimism about the quality of the American labor force misses a key fact: many of the Japanese cars are now made by American workers," Martin Feldstein, former chairman of the Council of Economic Advisers, observes. "In addition to their imports from Japan, the Japanese automakers are now turning out and selling nearly a million cars a year in the United States. American-made Japanese cars now account for nearly one out of every six U.S.–made cars — autos that are every bit as good and every bit as appealing as the autos made by Japanese workers."

Experts say the real reason for Japan's manufacturing edge is not advanced technology or low wages or some mystical Asian work ethic. Japan's most important advantage is its management system: the way it deals with employees, suppliers, dealers, and customers. Indeed, a recent MIT study of the world's auto companies concluded that Japan's superiority stems from a few simple elements: teamwork, efficient use of resources, and a tireless commitment to improving quality. Japanese manufacturers, for example, spend two thirds of their research and development budgets on process innovations, notes the Council on Competitiveness; U.S. manufacturers spend only one-third. Translation: the Japanese are always looking for new and better ways to make things.

In the final analysis, making things is what it's all about, and though in recent years we've taken great strides in making things well, we still have a long, long way to go. For example: I pull open the door of our American-made oven to retrieve a baking pan, and the plastic handle breaks off.

I fetch an apple from our new American-made refrigerator and discover that both plastic shelves above the vegetable bins are cracked — for the second time in less than a year.

I buy a box of galvanized finishing nails made by an American company. Almost half are already rusty, and many of the remaining nails are unusable because, in the galvanizing process, they were fused together.

I begin assembling a child's bureau produced by a factory in the South and find that several holes were drilled in the wrong places and that the laminated top is peeling apart.

Tired of stuffing tons of leaves into plastic trash bags every fall, I buy an electric leaf mulcher. The machine comes in a box with colorful photos and irresistible advertising claims, a box that also proudly proclaims, in big, bold letters, MADE IN THE U.S.A.

I begin assembling the mulcher on the living room floor. I carefully follow the instructions, and when it is halfway together, I suddenly realize I'm missing several parts. I search the box and the packing thoroughly, but the parts are nowhere to be found. I call the manufacturer's customer service department and describe the parts I need.

"I'll send you a new bag of parts," the woman on the other end says.

"But I don't need a whole new bag of parts," I say. "I just need the missing parts."

"This happens all the time," she replies brusquely. "It's easier for us to do it this way."

Several days later, I receive a new bag of parts, including the ones I need. The following weekend, I set up the mulcher next to a pile of leaves and eagerly plug it in. I drop in a batch of leaves, expecting them to be minced and quickly digested — just as it shows on the box. Instead, the mulcher instantly clogs. For the next half hour, I experiment with several techniques. Finally, I quit when I figure out that the only way to feed the mulcher without jamming it is to deposit no more than a handful of leaves at a time, meaning that I've paid nearly $100 for something that will make the onerous chore ten times more tedious than it was with a rake and bag.

I take the mulcher back to the store for a refund. The clerk tells me I'm the latest in a steady procession of dissatisfied customers. "Usually, people bring them back because the plastic housing cracks," he tells me.

MADE IN THE U.S.A., indeed.

Some might say I'm just unlucky, that I expect too much, that I take too much for granted and fail to appreciate all the good things America makes today. Arnold Packer of the Hudson Institute told me, "Frankly, I think the idea that things worked better in the good old days is a myth. I think American manufacturing has made substantial improvements and that most products today are *more* reliable. We have the ability to get in an automobile and travel a hundred thousand miles without the car overheating and breaking down. Our watches are accurate to the second for years. I work on a word processor — an incredibly sophisticated piece of machinery — and the damn thing works!

"Maybe the workmanship isn't as beautiful, but today's houses are better insulated, and the electrical and plumbing systems work better. Remember, in the old days, how hard it was to open a window? When you buy a big appliance, you expect it to work, and it usually does, and if it doesn't, it's covered by a warranty and you can get it fixed for nothing, or get a new one.

"Let's not kid ourselves: we do have a problem, but it's not because things have gone to hell in a handbasket. It's because the competition is stronger, the demands are greater, and the expectations are higher. It's not that Fords are worse than they used to be; it's that today Ford has to compete with Honda and Toyota."

Packer is correct. We do have to compete with Honda and Toyota — as well as Nissan and Suzuki and Isuzu, and BMW and Volkswagen and Mercedes-Benz, and Volvo and Saab and Jaguar, and on and on and on. But the difference now is that, instead of leading the way when it comes to quality, we are too often trailing — and forever scrambling just to catch up.

In my garage, I keep two Jeeps that were built by Willys-Overland Motors, of Toledo, Ohio, in 1948. I love these two vehicles, both for personal reasons (my grandfather had one when I was a kid) and because they are cultural artifacts, icons of American greatness, relics of a time when the United States made products the rest of the world admired and wanted.

My Jeeps have a distinguished pedigree. They are the direct civilian descendants of the jeep that helped win World War II — the flat-fendered, flat-hooded American classic that served valiantly in the North African deserts, in the South Pacific jungles, and on the Normandy beaches, earning the love of GIs and the respect of Patton, Marshall, and Eisenhower. The famed war correspondent Ernie Pyle once called the jeep "a divine instrument of military locomotion," and Enzo Ferrari praised it as "the only true American sports car." The jeep is a four-wheel sculpture of steel and sheet metal that the Museum of Modern Art, in 1951, declared a masterpiece of automotive design.

The basic jeep prototype was designed in 1940 by a patriotic engineer in a single weekend! The first jeep was constructed, from scratch, in only two months. The Army tested it mercilessly, driving it full tilt over log roads and plowed fields, through sapling forests and across sand traps, into a three-hundred-foot mud pit called "the hell hole," and off a four-foot loading platform, time and time again, at ten, then twenty, then thirty miles an hour. The jeep took all the punishment the quartermaster corps could dish out, and then some.

Later, during the war, the "steel soldier" was a true hero. With incredible maneuverability and speed, the jeep could go almost anywhere at any time and do almost anything when it got there. It could scoot for cover like a jack rabbit and travel across country like a deer. The jeep laid smoke screens and furnished hot radiator water for shaving. It was a machine gun mount and parade vehicle and reviewing stand. It served as a mobile command post, front-line ambulance, field telephone station, fire engine, railroad locomotive, and snow plow. It delivered fresh socks and C-rations, towed artillery and airplanes, and its broad hood was used as a map table, dining table, and altar for religious services.

Ernie Pyle wrote: "I don't think we could continue the war without the jeep. It does everything. It goes everywhere. It's as faithful as a dog, as strong as a mule, and as agile as a goat. All the time it carries loads twice as heavy as those it was designed for, and it keeps going just the same."

In the fifty years since its invention, the jeep has probably become the most famous car in the world, after Henry Ford's Model T. It is still hugely popular, because it symbolizes the scrappy, can-do, take-charge, four-wheel-drive spirit of a younger America, a nation that built things which were clever and tough and enduring.

That's not to say those older jeeps were perfect. They had a dangerously short wheel base, and often rolled over on curves. They forever leaked oil. They were noisy and smelly, and they got lousy mileage. Compared with today's Jeep Wrangler, which is manufactured by Chrysler, my ancient Willys Jeeps are primitive and puny.

So, as Packer rightly contends, there has been improvement. But quality is always relative. In their time, my Jeeps were remarkably innovative, high-quality vehicles, testaments to our country's industrial imagination and engineering prowess. But I'm not sure the same can be said about today's Jeep, for all its luxurious (and, in my opinion, inappropriate) appointments and all the modularized electronic gizmos that crowd its engine compartment (thus rendering it more complicated, more prone to inexplicable failure, and less easily fixed).

I recognize that U.S. carmakers have gotten religion and are trying to do a better job, but in today's universe of automobiles, the sad truth is that we still don't stack up. I have never owned an American car (except for those Jeeps and the '49 Plymouth coupe I drove as a senior in high school), and I can't say I regret it. From time to time, I've driven American cars — cars I've borrowed or cars I've rented — and I'm always amazed at how cheap and clunky and tinny they are.

I watch pro football on TV and see all the commercials for the new Fords and Chevies, Dodges and Chryslers, Buicks and Oldsmobiles, and I hear all the prattle about quality, quality, quality, and I look at the cars they're peddling, and I see the same boring, boxy shapes. Then I drive one of our new American company cars and it stalls out when I'm trying to accelerate onto the expressway, or the door handle comes off in my hand, or the emergency brake pedal falls apart, or I can't adjust the heater because the lever is missing, or the plastic glove box door won't close because the latch is jammed, or the seat isn't comfortable because the thin-gauge vinyl has cracked and ripped after less than a year of use.

Magazine ads for Buick brag about its being the only

American car company to finish in the top ten in an "initial quality" survey of 1990 models. Specifically, Buick finished in fifth place. Apparently, our standards are so low these days that this is something worth boasting about, that we have been beaten by *only four* foreign competitors (three Japanese, and one German, as it happens).

A newspaper item says that General Motors is recalling a whole batch of Pontiac Fieros because there's a chance the engines will catch on fire. How long have we been building cars, I ask myself. (Nearly a century, give or take a few years.) And the thought occurs: surely, with all our experience and all our gifted engineers and all our high-tech knowledge, we should be getting it right. By now, we should be making cars that are almost perfect, or at least cars with engines that won't burst into flames.

An older friend tells me he has just traded in his Lincoln Continental for a Lexus, Toyota's new luxury car. While we're trying to fix combustible engines, our Japanese competitors are taking automotive technology into the twenty-first century. My friend says his Lexus is the best car he's ever owned, bar none. When he drives it, the engine's so quiet that he often forgets the car is on, and the ride's so smooth and the handling so responsive that he sometimes feels he's no longer in contact with the road. "Take it out for a spin someday," he urges me. "It's an incredible experience. It will change your whole concept of cars and what driving can be like."

The word, apparently, is out. In little more than a year, Lexus has become phenomenally popular in the United States, beating both Mercedes-Benz and BMW. Significantly, more than a third of Lexus buyers traded in a Cadillac, Lincoln, or other American luxury cars to make their new purchase. Why? Because Lexus is, by all accounts, a vastly superior product. It incorporates some three hundred innovations, bristles with state-of-the-art luxuries, and is manufactured with fanatical attention to detail and quality. Toyota spent six years and more than $1 billion developing Lexus, and built 450 prototypes — three times the usual number — to perfect it.

But according to their standards, Toyota failed. Only three months after the highly acclaimed Lexus LS400 sedan was unveiled here, the company made an embarrassing announcement: all eight thousand cars it had sold were being recalled because of two consumer complaints, one about a defective brake light, the other about a sticky cruise-control mechanism. Within weeks, Lexus dealers contacted all eight thousand owners, made arrangements to pick up their cars, then swiftly repaired them, washed them, and returned them.

That's Toyota's definition of quality.

To me, the ultimate masterpieces of construction are the Gothic cathedrals in Europe. I've visited a few, and I'm always awestruck. I wonder about the anonymous artisans and laborers who built these magnificent edifices, patiently, carefully, exquisitely, working in stone — unyielding, permanent stone — over generations and centuries. These people clearly believed in an afterlife, in devoting themselves to something above and beyond themselves, something lasting and eternal.

Contemplating those cathedrals makes me wonder about us. What monuments to our faith are we leaving? The phallic, self-reflecting skyscrapers of Manhattan, sterile monuments to corporate ego, the quest for power, and the sanctity of the bottom line? The opulent shopping malls that necklace every major and minor settlement in America, strangling the vitality of Main Street? The ersatz Colonials crammed onto quarter-acre lots in exurban subdivisions with tally-ho names like "The Mews at Fox Run Chase"?

Over the years, because of an interest in construction as well as in land use and development, I've inspected many new houses. They are, in several respects, superior to the 200-year-old stone farmhouse I once owned and the 40-year-old stone-and-frame tract house I live in now. Some have cathedral ceilings and skylights and whirlpool bathtubs; some are enticing and attractive from the curb; but far too many of them are poorly situated, poorly built, and poorly finished.

I realize, of course, that labor and material costs have climbed to stratospheric levels and that houses can't be built the way they once were because they'd be far too costly for anyone but the superrich. But these new houses are not inexpensive: they sell for $200,000, $300,000, and up. And still they have leaky basements with walls made of porous cinder block. They have warped joists and stapled-together roof trusses and plastic pipes that rupture because they're insufficiently insulated or improperly installed. They have laminated wood floors that pull apart. They have exterior walls of flakeboard covered with vinyl siding that bubbles and bulges in hot weather. They have interior walls of plasterboard, hollow and easily perforated, as sturdy as a cereal box. Frequently, the joints, covered with paper strips and slathered with plaster, are so hastily sanded that the perimeter of every wallboard can be readily discerned.

As for trim, are there any finish carpenters left in America? For all the miraculous tools at their disposal, today's carpenters either don't have the skill to use them properly or — and this is more likely the case, in my opinion — they're too hurried and slipshod to turn out work that even remotely resembles craftsmanship. Around doors and windows, it is rare to see joints that meet perfectly. In the builders' rush to throw up houses faster and faster (some town-house developments seem to sprout from the ground overnight), everything is prefabricated, mass produced in factories, and hauled to the site. The lumber is green and rough. The molding stock is atrocious: short pieces of scrap glued together to form long strips that seem to get thinner and less substantial every year. Such quaint practices as countersinking finishing nails and puttying up the holes are as anachronistic as marble shower stalls and thick oak doors.

The decline of quality is evident not only in residential construction. Princeton's campus is deservedly regarded as one of the most beautiful in the country. The older, upper part of the campus consists almost entirely of hoary, ivy-covered stone buildings; it is a veritable museum of Colonial, Victorian, classical, and collegiate Gothic architecture. In the newer, lower part of the campus, stone yields to brick and, finally, poured concrete. Some of the university's newest buildings were designed by big-name architects and have won bigdeal awards, but in only a few short years they've acquired a dated, shabby look. Cement walks and walls are marred by fissures, paint is peeling off metal panels, fluorescent light fixtures dangle from suspended ceilings stained by leaks.

The new buildings were constructed to meet a need, to perform a function, to be as appealing as possible within the university's increasingly straitened budget. But these postmodern fabrications also have an agenda: to celebrate the capabilities of contemporary building materials, to expand the boundaries of architectural expression, to promote a certain architect's theories, to advance a particular movement or school of thought, to advertise the avant-garde, to make a cultural statement.

The cognoscenti may find these buildings thrilling and inspiring. To me they are cold and stark. They do not compare with the university's older buildings, which have the aura of history and tradition, which signify a heritage, the continuity of civilized values, and the specialness of the university and its mission. The newer buildings are posturing upstarts, embodiments of jarring abstractions. They neither soothe the soul nor lift the spirit. They are merely unpleasant reminders of the esthetic bankruptcy of the modern age, of the pervasive tawdriness of modern construction, of the general decline in quality and in the quality of life.

On the campus of the University of Pennsylvania, there is a pedestrian bridge that arches over a busy street. It is a graceful concrete span used by hundreds of students as they travel between their dorms and classes. In recent years, however, the bridge has become pocked as chunks of concrete flake off. Whenever I see that bridge, I think of my grandfather and his perennial complaints about the flagstone walkway in front of his house. His walkway is forever breaking up, no matter how often it's repaired. "What gives?" my grandfather asks. "Why is it the ancient Romans could build intricate and magnificent stone structures like aqueducts that are still standing nearly two thousand years later? What did their masons know that we don't?"

My grandfather's favorite skyscraper is the Woolworth Building in New York City. Built in the early years of this century, it is a soaring, stately edifice, dignified by Gothic Revival adornments, pleasing in its symmetry and proportion. It is truly a beautiful building, a majestic work of art, and it stands in dramatic contrast to most of Manhattan's newer skyscrapers — monotonous steel-and-glass boxes as anonymous in character as the corporate grovelers who process paper inside them.

I can imagine what some of you are thinking.

You've probably decided that I'm a reactionary, a retrograde romantic who believes everything was better in the good old days. You're thinking I'm one of those unrealistic people who pine for a prelapsarian past that never was and is offended by anything new, anything foreign to my hopelessly nostalgic vision of yesteryear — a vision that exists only in my sentimental imagination.

I'll concede this much: I am a romantic and I do have

great respect for the past. But I'm also aware of how good and wonderful the present is. If given a choice between living today or in 1950 or 1930 or 1920 or the nineteenth or eighteenth century, I'd certainly stay where I am right now. Just in terms of conveniences and technological advances, I'd have to give up too much if I went back. Moreover, in many ways — social justice, for one — America is a much better place today than it was, say, fifty or a hundred years ago.

But as much as I appreciate the glories of the present and the remarkable progress we've made, I can't ignore what I see and hear. And what I see and hear is not comforting. What I see and hear points to how much the past *was* superior to the present. What I see and hear convinces me that quality — in people, work, products, service, art, architecture, music, you name it — is becoming rarer by the day.

I sit on a commuter train behind a group of four boys. They are having an animated conversation. Every other word is *motherfucker*, which they use without the slightest emotion or compunction. It seems to be a synonym for *person* or *guy*.

I spin the radio dial one morning and come across shock jock Howard Stern. He is trying to talk a young female guest into taking off her shirt, and she, in turn, wants him to pull down his pants. This is now one of the most popular radio programs in New York and Philadelphia.

I buy a tan summer suit at Brooks Brothers, famous for lofty prices, preppy stodginess, and old-fashioned quality. I wear it three or four times and discover that the lining is separating from the jacket and the fabric around the collar is unraveling.

I turn on the car radio and hear a "song" that's apparently climbing the charts. The lyrics are basically three words: "It feels good." These words are moaned with a lazy, lascivious suggestiveness, over and over again, for three or four minutes. Will this mindless anthem of modern love evoke memories of romance thirty or forty years from now? I wonder. Or will today's teenagers recall the tender moments of their youth by listening to the Dead Kennedys sing "I Kill Children" or W.A.S.P. sing "Fuck Like a Beast" or Ozzy Osbourne sing "Bloodbath in Paradise"?

I am stopped by a policeman, who gives me a warning ticket for driving with a defective headlight. I'm told to fix the headlight within forty-eight hours and verify the repair at the police station. I do so. A clerk stamps my ticket, smiles, and says everything's taken care of. One month later, I receive a summons from the local magistrate, notifying me that I must pay an $85 fine for ignoring the warning ticket. The woman I talk to at the police station is sympathetic.

"It was probably a computer glitch," she says.

"What can be done about it?" I ask.

"Nothing," she says. "You'll have to go to court. It's in the computer now."

I receive a letter from the chairman and chief executive officer of a major American company. It has been typed by his secretary. In the letter, the word *Monday* is "Momnday," the word *anecdote* is "antidote," the word *decline* is "deline," the word *intact* is "in tact," and two sentences are missing so many words that they are completely unintelligible.

I hear everyone at the office buzzing about David Lynch's TV series, *Twin Peaks.* They are intelligent, sensible people whose opinions I respect. I decide to watch an episode to see what all the fuss is about. What I see are bizarre, twisted characters leading lives of stylized depravity. It is nasty, sociopathic tripe, steeped in nightmarish malevolence, self-consciously abstruse, and dolled up to look like art — which makes it permissible viewing, I suppose, for putative sophisticates.

I visit the Philadelphia Museum of Art to check out the hot new juried exhibition "Contemporary Philadelphia Artists." Among the masterpieces I see are several bricks arranged in a curve, a raggedy latex jacket and pair of pants, what looks like a souped-up wire trash basket without a bottom, a rod from which a tangle of filament hangs, a piece of paper with an underlined *y* on it, and a video "installation" featuring three TV sets, one of which beams question marks at the viewer — an appropriate symbol for the whole experience

I pick up *Esquire* and discover that the magazine which once published Fitzgerald and Hemingway has now become a fatter version of The Sharper Image catalogue. It is full of slick ads for men's cologne, Ralph Lauren clothes, sleek cars, digitalized audio equipment, and all sorts of other gadgets that the yupscale male needs to sate his materialistic impulses, tone his physique, and woo the woman of the week. In between are didactic little essays that strive mightily to combat modern anomie by telling the rough-edged man on the make how to dress, how to look, how to act, and how to think. The Great American Novelist featured in this particular issue is Philip Roth. His offering here, an excerpt from his novel *Deception*, is an onanistic fantasy about adultery, a self-absorbed bit of literary sleight-of-hand that, after a few pages, seems dismissibly slight of mind.

I peruse the latest masterpiece by Bret Easton Ellis, celebrated exponent of yuppie nihilism and despair. His new novel, *American Psycho*, is about a Wall Street investment banker who vents his rage by torturing and mutilating women — with nail gun, power drill, chain saw, and in one scene a ravenous rat. Simon & Schuster, the book's original publisher, paid Ellis a $300,000 advance for this valuable contribution to American literature. But after embarrassing prepublication publicity, they dumped it. Not to worry. Vintage Books, a division of Random House, scooped it right up. It was, after all, a matter of defending artistic freedom. Besides, as one book editor noted, Ellis is a "brilliant" writer. A sample from *American Psycho:* "I start by skinning Torri a little, making incisions with a steak knife and ripping bits of flesh from her legs and stomach while she screams in vain, begging for mercy in a high thin voice . . . I keep spraying Torri with Mace and then I try to cut off her fingers with nail scissors and finally I pour acid onto her belly and genitals, but none of this comes close to killing her, so I resort to stabbing her in the throat and eventually the blade of the knife breaks off in what's left of her neck, stuck on the bone, and I stop. While Tiffany watches, finally I saw the entire head off — torrents of blood splash against the walls, even the ceiling — and holding the head up, like a prize, I take my cock, purple with stiffness, and lowering Torri's head to my lap, I push it into her bloodied mouth and start fucking it, until I come, exploding into it."

There are other passages that are even more vile, but not so vile that they prevented the book from leaping onto the best-seller list. Sure to become a major motion picture. Count on it.

What's wrong with us? Why are we tolerating so much that is shallow and superficial, cheap and meretricious, sloppy and shoddy? Why have we permitted quality to deteriorate in so many spheres of modern life?

Part of the reason is our ambivalence about the idea of quality itself. Quality implies standards, and we Americans have always been suspicious of standards. Standards imply discrimination — making decisions about what is better, what is best — selection, and, possibly, exclusion. The setting of standards militates against our bedrock belief in egalitarianism. It smacks of elitism — the most heinous of democratic sins, especially at a time when all moral and cultural values are deemed to be relative.

Equal rights and equal opportunity are admirable principles of state, but egalitarianism, as interpreted and understood today, is a form of good-hearted wish fulfillment that violates natural law. Way back in the eighteenth century, Montesquieu saw political egalitarianism as a "dangerous fallacy" that could lead only to incompetence — and, he added, mob rule.

The late historian Barbara Tuchman, in a *New York Times Magazine* essay entitled "The Decline of Quality," noted sorrowfully that "the new egalitarians would like to make the whole question of quality vanish by adopting a flat philosophy of the equality of everything. No factor or event is of greater or less value than any other; no person or thing is superior or inferior to any other. Any reference to quality is instantly castigated as elitism, which seems to inspire in users of the word the sentiments of Jacobins denouncing aristos to the guillotine. In fact, elitism is the equivalent of quality. Without it, management of everything would be on a par with the United States Postal Service, which, mercifully, is not yet quite the case. Difference in capacity does exist, and superiority makes itself felt. It wins the ski race and promotion on the job and admission to the college of its choice. There are A students and D students, and their lives and fortunes will be different."

Quality implies inequality; it implies difference and distinction; it implies rank and an order of worth, value, and achievement. Quality is occasionally cruel and Darwinian: survival of the fittest, only the strong shall thrive, the cream rises to the top. It is the product of excellence, and it flourishes only when excellence is honored.

"Now that the pejorative 'elitist' is used to denounce advocates of excellence, excellence, inevitably, will become scarcer," William Manchester, the biographer and historian, wrote in a newspaper essay. "The language is deteriorating in the name of 'usage,' under which grammar is determined by a kind of continuing voice vote: if sufficient people say, 'I feel badly,' or 'It is me,' the error ceases to be an error."

We live in an age, it seems, when we're expected to look down on those above us, and up to those beneath us. "Since superiority is in itself suspect, everyone tries to look like, talk like, and be like everyone else," observed Manchester, "and thus all the attributes that once separated people from one another are discounted. Doubtless this comforts those in whose breasts lurks the gnawing (and usually justified) hunch that they really are inferior. It puts extraordinary souls at a disadvantage, however, and it is they, not the dross of society, who will determine the direction of the road, whether it be high or low, and whether the journey will even be completed."

Unfortunately, in our eagerness to embrace "diversity" and "pluralism," to erase all the *isms* of the past, to be tolerant, "sensitive," and "nonjudgmental," we have created a new secular religion. Its name is Openness, and its fundamental dogma is an unqualified acceptance of anybody and everybody, anything and everything. All moral judgments are strictly subjective; right or wrong, good or bad, it's all in the eye of the perpetrator.

Such a philosophy not only excuses incompetence but also leads to the rejection of norms, the breakdown of law and order, and the collapse of society into anarchy. "Openness — and the relativism that makes it the only plausible stance in the face of various claims to truth and various ways of life and kinds of human beings — is the great insight of our times," wrote Allan Bloom in *The Closing of the American Mind*. "It is progressive and forward-looking. It does not demand fundamental agreement or the abandonment of old or new beliefs . . . It is open to all kinds of men, all kinds of lifestyles, all ideologies. There is no enemy other than the man who is not open to everything. But when there are no shared goals or vision of the public good, is the social contract any longer possible?"

Openness sounds nice and is nice and wants to be nice, and in the eyes of many nice people, it seems to make perfect sense. The problem is that openness is inimical to quality, because it insists on indiscriminateness. Why? Because the opposite of indiscriminateness is — egads! — *discrimination.* "This folly means that men are not permitted to seek for the natural human good and admire it when found," explained Bloom, "for such discovery is coeval with the discovery of the bad and contempt for it."

A society afraid to acknowledge the best because it's afraid to acknowledge the worst is a society where quality is doomed. Such a society may continue to survive, but it will never advance, for a sense of quality is essential to any nation that aspires to progress. Honoring quality means being aware of the highest, and being aware of the highest means having something to reach for. Put another way, a society afraid of excellence should not be surprised by incompetence.

8 What Do We Do Now?

VIETNAM is the shameful war the United States lost, the war that demonstrated American military incompetence. World War II, of course, is the glorious war the United States won, the war that demonstrated American military competence. Or so goes the romantic myth.

Actually, both wars were characterized by horrendous mistakes, monstrous stupidity, and staggering waste, of both men and matériel. But somehow, perhaps because the cause was just and the outcome different from that of Vietnam, the ineptitude so prevalent in World War II has been glossed over, covered up, and overlooked. Veterans have edited their memories, forgetting the outrageous errors, the accidental sacrifices, the needless loss of life and limb. In some cases, rationalizing historians have performed cosmetic surgery, prettying up the record for posterity.

The truth is, World War II was not so glorious after all. "The Americans and British committed many more blunders than the Germans or the Japanese," wrote Paul Fussell in *Wartime: Understanding and Behavior in the Second World War.* "Blunders were almost the hallmark of Allied operations."

Some examples reported by Fussell:

▶ *During the invasion of Sicily in 1943, American naval and ground gunners panicked and shot down twenty-*

three transport planes and gliders, blasting 229 men of the 82nd Airborne Division out of the sky.

▶ *During the Normandy invasion in 1944, many U.S. planes goofed and dropped their bombs a day early. They were also off-target; twenty-five American soldiers were killed and 131 wounded. Some American units were so enraged that they opened fire on their own aircraft.*

The next day, the bombing was even wilder, wiping out 111 GIs and injuring 500. "Men were torn apart," wrote Fussell, "tanks were tossed around like toys, and troops were driven insane."

▶ *In July 1945, the United States heavy cruiser* Indianapolis *was sunk by a Japanese submarine. The Navy brass didn't realize for four days that the vessel was overdue. By then, five hundred men had died on rafts or in life jackets — from thirst, hunger, madness, and shark bites. It was, wrote Fussell, "the greatest loss of life at sea ever suffered by the United States."*

All of this is meant to underscore an important point: incompetence has always existed and always will (as will ardent lamentations about it). The annals of the past spill over with pitiful examples; the present has no monopoly.

Indeed, incompetence is a permanent feature of the human condition. It is human to err, to make mistakes, to cause accidents. What distinguishes ordinary human fallibility from incompetence, however, is the element of deliberateness. In most cases, incompetence is a failure of will, a conscious decision not to do what ought to be done, not to try, not to take the extra step, not to give it your very best. Typically, incompetence results from hastiness, carelessness, sloppiness, and laziness.

Whether incompetence is worse now than before is really academic. What counts is the perception. And the perception for far too many Americans is that incompetence is growing, outstripping the best efforts of the capable and diligent, who are burdened with the terrible fear that our best days are behind us and that this great nation has begun its inevitable descent.

That loss of faith, particularly among the nation's best and brightest, has become a serious problem in itself, compounding the damages of incompetence. As Richard Critchfield wrote in *An American Looks at Britain*, a book about the decline of British culture, "Any society's loss of faith — in life, in the world, in the spiritual, in itself — can affect everything: how hard people work, how inventive they are, how much initiative they take, in short, their enterprise."

Already, the effects are all too evident. Incompetence is so ubiquitous in the United States that it is sapping our economy, hampering our ability to compete, threatening our well-being, impinging on our quality of life, and breaching the social contract. Slowly, the bonds of trust that are essential to the survival and progress of any society are beginning to unravel.

What can we do? Are we doomed to a future of decline? Can we fix America and restore it to its former greatness? In short, is there any hope? You bet there is. This nation certainly has the skill and talent and resources to undertake and conquer nearly any challenge. The only question is: Do we have the will?

Happily, for every example of incompetence in this country, you can still find ten examples of competence. It's a testament to our innate optimism that the screw-ups and failures usually grab our attention and capture the headlines, because screw-ups and failures still strike us Americans as exceptional and extraordinary, newsworthy departures from the norm.

All across the land, there are outstanding examples of American excellence. Remember: we're the nation that produced Joe Montana, the nearly infallible quarterback of the San Francisco 49ers. We've given the world the peerless actress Meryl Streep. IBM, Xerox, and RCA, not exactly slouches to begin with, are hustling with the best of them. Maybe our postal service isn't so hot, but we've got Federal Express and United Parcel Service (have you ever seen a dirty UPS truck?). And if you're feeling depressed about the quality of American service, just dial 1-800-221-4221. That's the toll-free number of L. L. Bean, where you can order high-quality outdoor goods from real human beings who are intelligent, courteous, knowledgeable, and genuinely helpful. We've also got Walt Disney World, that immaculate, fantastically efficient showcase of our entertainment genius and imagination. Last, but hardly least, the masterminds of Operation Desert Storm — Dick Cheney, Colin Powell, and Norman Schwarzkopf — were *our guys*, and those Patriot missiles that knocked out Saddam's Scuds and those laser-guided bombs that hit their targets with such stunning accuracy were made not in Japan or Korea or Taiwan, but right here in the U.S. of A.

Another encouraging sign is that we know something's wrong with us. America has a long tradition of self-examination and self-criticism that for the most part has been salutary. I'm not the first to sound the themes enunciated in this book; there's been sporadic talk about declining competence and quality for at least a decade. And some of that talk has resulted in action — action that's beginning to pay off.

Detroit has shed some of its hubris and begun taking lessons from the competition. In brainstorming how to organize the plant that would manufacture its innovative Saturn automobile, for example, General Motors assembled the Group of 99, a team of Saturn workers who traveled two million miles and investigated some 160 pioneering enterprises, including Hewlett-Packard, McDonald's, Volvo, Kawasaki, and Nissan.

Thanks to such initiatives, GM, and Ford and Chrysler too, now make cars that are better and higher in quality than those they built in the 1960s and 1970s. Today, many Europeans, even the picky Swiss, buy U.S. automobiles.

The Japanese have been promoting quality in business and industry for years by giving out the Deming Prize, named after W. Edwards Deming. In 1987, the U.S. Congress decided that what works for Japan might work for us and established the Malcolm Baldrige National Quality Award, named for the Commerce Secretary who died while the legislation creating the prize was being debated. "American business and industry are beginning to understand that poor quality costs companies as much as 20 percent of sales revenues nationally," declared the act instituting the award, "and that improved quality of goods and services goes hand in hand with improved productivity, lower costs, and increased profitability."

Corporate America, with its red-blooded fondness for home runs and touchdowns, likes the Baldrige contest. The number of companies asking for applications — now running in the thousands — grows dramatically each year. Scores of businesses have had enough confidence in the quality of what they're making and doing to go after the honor — a quest that entails months of rigorous analysis and documentation. All this has further spread the consciousness of quality and has improved attitudes, workmanship, products, and services.

In 1990, the Cadillac Motor Car Division of General Motors won one of the crystal "Baldriges," along with IBM Rochester, of Rochester, Minnesota; Federal Express, of Memphis; and the Wallace Company, a small industrial-plumbing company of Houston. In accepting the award, the Cadillac general manager, John Grettenberger, spoke of the remarkable changes at Cadillac, which lost thousands of customers in the early 1980s because of cheaply built, underpowered, downsized automobiles that were rejected by luxury-car buyers. "What we learned really resulted in a total transformation in the way we do business," Grettenberger said, adding that the firm's revival was based on the not-so-innovative strategies of teamwork and customer satisfaction. Workers at the Detroit assembly plant where many Caddies are built agree. "We are actually calling Cadillac owners and asking their opinions," said UAW member Bill Howey. "Some of the things that we have drawn out of them have led to specific changes in the car, such as map holders behind the seats."

Another positive factor is that the American Dream still shines brightly for most of the world. The diversity of people in America makes for a roilsome, chaotic, contentious society — a society where there's frequently a lot of pushing and shoving and throwing of elbows — but it is also the marrow of our greatness, the wellspring of our strength. As the management consultant and educator Peter Drucker remarked to *U.S. News & World Report*, "The great advantage of a highly pluralistic society is that there's a lot of local experimentation going on, and you don't wait for a minister of education, or a manager or professor. You experiment. You make a lot of errors, and maybe something comes out that works."

This nation of immigrants has always relied on new citizens to renew and invigorate itself, and these new Americans, fortunately, are still coming. Asian-Americans and Asian immigrants now make up 28 percent of the freshman class at Berkeley, although they represent fewer than 9 percent of California's high school graduates. "I see Vietnamese and Korean fruit vendors who run their businesses incredibly competently," says Ross A. Webber of the Wharton School. "I'm impressed by the amazing vitality of the Cubans in Miami. The genius of the American system is our ability to attract the most competent and most ambitious people. It's been true for 150 years and there's been no diminution in that attractiveness. The immigration of bright people will continue to be the dynamic that lifts all our aspirations."

For all their recent success, even the Japanese envy and

admire the United States. Japan is still very much a rich country full of poor people. In this tiny island nation, people are cramped, the cost of living is astronomical, and real estate is so expensive that it's virtually out of reach, except for the very rich. Compared with the average Japanese family, the typical middle-class American family, living in a split-level, with two cars in the driveway and perhaps a back-yard swimming pool and power boat, lives like royalty.

Moreover, Japanese society is rigid and authoritarian. The strict discipline that helped make Japan an economic powerhouse has bred a society that, by American standards, can be insufferably repressive, intolerant, and inhumane. Perhaps you remember the furor that was caused in July 1990 when a fifteen-year-old Japanese schoolgirl, only seconds late for class, was crushed to death as she tried to scamper past a five-hundred-pound iron gate that was shoved closed by a teacher intent on reducing tardiness.

The Japanese know we've got problems galore, but they're still irresistibly attracted to America — our wide-open spaces, our independence, our energy, our vitality, our creativity, our glamour, our zaniness and insouciance and naïveté, and, of course, our huge market of insatiable and relatively prosperous consumers. Japanese youth worship American movie stars and pop culture heroes. They scramble for tickets to witness Madonna's delicious decadence, and Tom Cruise is a bigger sex symbol in Tokyo than he is in Los Angeles. Satin warmup jackets that say SAN FRANCISCO 49ERS, OAKLAND A's, or L.A. LAKERS — the Japanese love winners — are part of the uniform worn by hip Japanese teenagers. Many Japanese may have more faith in the United States than a lot of Americans do. And though they may chafe at our carping and growing laziness, they are investing in the United States at record levels. According to a recent *Newsweek* poll, only 16 percent of Japanese believe the United States is in "irreversible decline."

Want some more good news?

For all their vaunted productivity, it takes a Japanese worker an hour to produce what an American can in thirty-one minutes, noted *The Economist*. In 1950, regarded by many as the peak of our economic golden age, U.S. gross national product was $1.6 trillion (in current dollars). GNP today is $5.5 trillion — two times bigger than Japan's and five times larger than Germany's. As for individual welfare, per capita GNP is now more than twice what it was at the century's midpoint, those seemingly halcyon days when America was basking in postwar prosperity and looking forward to having likable Ike in the White House.

In the last fifteen years, America's Fortune 500 companies lost fifteen million jobs, but the U.S. economy has *added* forty-five million jobs, and factory output jumped 30 percent since 1980. "The large companies in this country do not matter anymore," said Drucker in his interview. "A few have regained momentum, but the economy has shifted to the medium-sized, highly concentrated concerns." In other words, megacorporations like General Motors are no longer as important to the economy as are smaller, more focused companies that supply, say, special parts to GM and other giants around the nation and the world.

As for our trade deficit? It has "absolutely nothing to do either with Japanese prowess or with American manufacturing incompetence," according to Drucker. "Our trade deficit is, sadly, the result of the collapse of raw-material prices. The U.S. is the world's largest exporter of raw materials and food. If our 1988 volume had been what it was 10 years earlier, 40 percent of the trade deficit would have been wiped out."

Many of the new employment "opportunities" created during the Reagan era were moronic, minimum-wage, hamburger-flipping jobs, but much of the work in modern service-industry America is far more pleasant and interesting than what smokestack America had to offer. "We're developing an industrial romance, just as we used to have a romance about the farmer," says Larry Hirschhorn, of the Wharton Center for Applied Research. "We're beginning to romanticize about what it was like to work in the big steel mills once upon a time, where Real Men did Real Work and made Real Things. In fact, those jobs were hot, sweaty, backbreaking, and dangerous. Personally, I think it's a good thing that we're going to a service economy, an information-based economy. People now have a chance to do more intelligent work."

I hope this makes you feel a little bit better — enough so that you aren't paralyzed by despair, but not so much that you forget what you've read in the rest of the book. Plainly, we cannot afford to feel self-satisfied and complacent. As John Brademas, the president of New York University, said in a speech at DePauw University in June 1990, "We must face up to the gap between Western values, American values — individual freedoms, democratic politics, competitive markets — and reality in our country. While people long oppressed risk their lives to take part in protests or cast ballots, less than half of those eligible to vote in the United States bother to do so. And while one country after another breaks away from command economies, our own economic independence is more and more threatened by our need to borrow."

In other words, we've been coasting for far too long, squandering the moral, political, and economic capital that made this nation a beacon of excellence. We are now at a crucial juncture, and how we respond will determine whether we hold our own in the competitive world of the twenty-first century or slide into bankruptcy, decay, and oblivion.

What can we do?

The natural impulse is to say: They (*they* meaning the government, of course) ought to (fill in the blank) _____.

► *quit meddling abroad and playing global cop and pay more attention to our tremendous problems back home;*

► *stop buying so many war toys for the boys in the Pentagon and use those precious tax dollars instead to help the poor, rebuild our decaying cities, rejuvenate mass transit, and make America "a kinder, gentler nation";*

► *limit the terms of congressmen, cap what they can spend on their election campaigns, and ban contributions from corporations, lobbyists, and special-interest groups;*

► *halt those damn federal deficits by passing a constitutional amendment requiring a balanced budget;*

► *pay more than lip service to the importance of the family by providing more money, services, and programs, such as fully subsidized day care for the children of working parents;*

► *spend even more millions on schools and boost salaries even higher to attract better teachers;*

► *change the tax laws so that they penalize people for spending and reward people for saving and investing;*

► *change the tax laws so that they reward corporations for long-range planning, research, and development;*

► *slap trade restrictions on all those underpriced Japanese imports that are wiping out American jobs;*

▶ *bust the unions, or bust the companies that bust the unions, depending on your point of view;*

▶ *reform the tort-law industry by limiting liability awards and enacting stiff criminal penalties for phony claims and the ambulance chasers who encourage them;*

▶ *outlaw corporate takeovers, junk bonds, and anybody under forty who works on Wall Street and wears suspenders;*

▶ *establish a national apprenticeship program or a system of professional training academies, supported by private industry, to teach skills, instill a sense of pride, and foster a positive work ethic;*

▶ *set up a national institute to monitor and regulate product quality . . .*

And so on and so on. Feel free to write in your own bright ideas, nostrums, and panaceas, but remember: you're a fool if you expect much from the federal government, because the government is largely responsible for getting us into this mess in the first place. Besides, the malignancy I've conveniently termed incompetence is so basic and systemic that attacking it in a formal, organized fashion (petitions, marches on Washington, sit-ins at the Capitol to protest incompetence — now there's an intriguing thought) would be of little or no use. It would be nifty, even as just a PR gesture, if the President declared war on incompetence and established a blue-ribbon National Commission on Competence and launched some kind of Marshall Plan to develop and promote competence. But aside from the ludicrousness and hypocrisy of the nitwits in Washington — the capital of ineptitude and moral flaccidity — spearheading such a campaign (Who would be its chairman? Dan Quayle? Gerald Ford? Warren Burger? Jesse Helms? Oh, wait . . . Lee Iacocca, of course), such an approach is guaranteed to fail.

Why? Because, in the final analysis, *they* is really *we*. Or, in the immortal words of the cartoon character Pogo, "We has met the enemy, and it is us." Incompetence can't be rooted out from the top down; it must be eradicated from the bottom up. Incompetence is an infraction of what political scientists call civic virtue. In order for a society to cohere and function, people must share certain duties, certain values, certain loyalties, certain habits of mind, certain qualities of heart. A good citizen, for example, should be kind; a good citizen should try hard; a good citizen should do a full day's work for a full day's pay; a good citizen should assist the weak and infirm; a good citizen should care for children and the aged; a good citizen should pull over to the side of the road to let an ambulance pass; a good citizen should vote; a good citizen should fill out his census forms; a good citizen should be honest in business; a good citizen should be faithful to family and friends.

Such behavior cannot be legislated; civic virtue — so vital in a democracy — requires what one writer has called "obedience to the unenforceable." No government, no social program, no outside force can make anyone do these things. You have to want to do them, of your own free will, because you wish to contribute to the greater good, and because you realize that if you don't, you'll cut yet another thread in the social fabric — and, ultimately, jeopardize your own well-being and prospects for survival.

The bad news about incompetence is that it's one of those abstract, amorphous social ailments that are so pervasive that they make the efforts of a single person seem futile. The good news about incompetence is that it begins and ends with individuals. Incompetent people propagate incompetence; competent people propagate competence. Incompetence and competence are highly contagious, each emanating through society like ripples on a placid lake.

Incompetence is primarily an attitude. No one, except those who are physically and mentally impaired, is born incompetent. Incompetence is an acquired characteristic, instilled and fostered by the moral environment. The operative word here is *moral*, for incompetence is essentially a moral problem, in the original, most fundamental sense of the Latin word *mores*, meaning "customs" or "manners."

Incompetence flourishes because we accept it and tolerate it. It thrives because of silence and apathy. It feeds on moral cowardice, on what Christopher Lasch, a history professor at the University of Rochester and the author of *The Culture of Narcissism*, describes as "the mistaken idea that moral issues are purely subjective and personal and therefore there's no point in talking about them. There's a tremendous fear of disagreement today. People believe that serious disagreement is likely to lead to trouble, and so this puts a premium on avoiding any issues that might be divisive or controversial."

So the "cure" for incompetence is a resurgence of moral bravery. We must overcome our fear of offending, our pathological eagerness to be considered nice or hip or politically correct. We must not be afraid to insist on quality, to assert and defend standards of excellence, to condemn incompetence in all its manifestations. "The only thing necessary for the triumph of evil is for good men to do nothing," Edmund Burke once wrote. His admonition applies to incompetence as well.

Today, among some self-styled sophisticates, even the mention of morals raises eyebrows and causes smirks of derision. Upholding moral principles is viewed as a gross breach of ideological etiquette. It stigmatizes you as uncool, unenlightened, and worse — a prig, a bigot, a fascist. *Mind your own business. It's my life and I'll live it the way I want. What are you, anyway, some kind of self-righteous troglodyte?* This attitude, popularized by the drug-besotted heavy thinkers of the morally plastic Woodstock Generation, is epitomized by the idiotic exhortation "Do your own thing," a licentious credo that has helped make us what we are today — a sick, uncouth, fragmented society that has lost its moral compass and the core values necessary to hold the nation together. "The things that will destroy America are prosperity at any price, safety-first instead of duty-first, the love of soft living and the get-rich-quick theory of life," Theodore Roosevelt once wrote. "Americanism is a test of spirit and conviction and purpose, not of creed or birthplace. The world has set its face hopefully toward our democracy. The test of our worth is the service we render."

Yeats warns in one of his poems that a society must not disintegrate into randomness; there must be a cultural and ethical tradition that binds us all. The historian Kenneth Clark says that civilization, distilled to a single word, is manners — by which he means self-respect expressed as respect for others (a definition that could aptly apply to competence). A civilized society demands consideration for others; it demands that self-interest be transcended and sublimated for the common weal. Yes, freedom and liberty should be enshrined, and individual rights should be duly asserted and protected. But, as Alexander Solzhenitsyn has observed, "It is time, in the West, to defend not so much human rights as human obligations."

It is time, in other words, for more responsibility. "In every institution in our society, be it religious, health, educational, legal, or military, it always seems to be the most recalcitrant and the least motivated that are calling the shots," said Edwin H. Friedman, a family therapist, in *Family Therapy News*. A former rabbi who was a community relations specialist for the White House during the early days of the civil rights movement, Friedman says that everywhere he goes he hears the same complaints: "The dependents are in charge. The adaptation is in the wrong direction. A disproportionate amount of time, energy, money, and concern is being spent on those who will do the least with it. The strengths of our species are being diluted by focus on pathology. Not the meek but the weak are inheriting the earth. It's counter-evolutionary."

Counter-evolutionary and, from the standpoint of America's health, potentially lethal. That is why we must do something now.

Where to begin?

Right where you are. Voltaire was correct when he declared, *Il faut cultiver notre jardin* — "We must cultivate our garden." Or, as the bumper sticker says, THINK GLOBALLY. ACT LOCALLY. "Never doubt that a small group of thoughtful, committed citizens can change the world," anthropologist Margaret Mead once observed. "Indeed, it's the only thing that ever has." In the battle against incompetence, you alone can make a difference, in your own humble sphere of influence, by doing two things: being as competent yourself as you can be, and demanding quality and competence from everything and everybody you deal with every day.

In other words, don't settle for less. Don't settle for inferior effort or inferior work or inferior products — from anybody. And yes, it's OK to express moral outrage. Not only OK but necessary. In fact, you should turn up the flame of outrage and lower your threshold for moral insult. In the fight against incompetence, it's time to play hardball. You should become what a friend of mine calls an "urban Rambo" — ruthless in flushing out and flaying incompetence, for your own satisfaction as well as the protection of those who must deal with that person or organization after you. (Likewise, when you encounter work, effort, or products that are *superior*, praise the provider lavishly to encourage and perpetuate such excellence.)

Has the vacuum cleaner you bought only three months ago already broken? Take it back. Ask for a refund. Call or write to the manufacturer and tell the company how lousy their product is. Tell them they ought to be ashamed.

Did your waiter take forty-five minutes to serve you, screw up your order, and act surly to boot? For God's sake, don't leave a tip. But tell him why — and let the restaurant manager know as well.

Did that gum-popping receptionist make you wait fifteen minutes while she gabbed with a girlfriend on the phone? Let her know you're annoyed, and raise holy hell with her supervisor.

Are your political representatives all nincompoops and crooks? Don't just sit in front of the tube and stew in your own impotence. You have a franchise. Get out and vote. Get your friends and neighbors to vote. Organize your own grass-roots movement and throw the bums out.

Yes, it takes some effort and occasionally some courage, but in the end it will be well worth it, even if you don't get a refund or elect your candidate or change the world overnight.

Why? Because there is no dignity or majesty in life unless we strive: to make the bad good, the good better, and the better best. As the author Leo Rosten has written: "Most men debase the 'pursuit of happiness' by transforming it into a narcotic pursuit of 'fun.' But there are those sublimely cursed by discontent, and to them happiness comes only when they push their brains and hearts to the farthest reaches of which they are capable. Nothing is more rewarding than the effort a man makes to matter — to count, to stand for something, to have it make some difference that he lived at all."

So we can — and we must — make a stand against incompetence. We owe it to ourselves. We owe it to those who have gone before us. But much more, we owe it to those who will come after. Too many are depending on us, and too much is at stake, for us to surrender America to the enemies of effort, achievement, and civilization.

Acknowledgments

At the risk of undercutting the premise of this book, I wish to salute the contributions of numerous people who are exceptionally competent.

This book began as an article in the *Philadelphia Inquirer Magazine*. There wouldn't have been a book if there hadn't been a magazine article. And there wouldn't have been an article if it hadn't been for Avery Rome, the magazine's managing editor. It was she who suggested the idea, gently nudged me to write about it, then adroitly transformed my original draft into a provocative polemic that had focus, bite, and punch.

I never could have undertaken the project without the backing of Fred Mann, the editor of the *Inquirer Magazine*, who generously accommodated the writing ambitions of this reluctant editor and who gave me the time and freedom to explore the subject with the care and thoroughness it deserved. I'm much indebted also to several other magazine colleagues — Sue Weston, Bill Eddins, Tom Frail, and Charles Layton — whose constructive criticism and sharp-eyed proofreading made the article about as flawless as is humanly possible. In addition, art director Bert Fox's imaginative design and eye-catching display captured the gist of the piece. Staff artist Earl Davis did splendid work on the reprint, and Sally Downey distributed hundreds of copies to clamorous readers with her usual cheerful efficiency (while nimbly shielding me from all manner of pests, crackpots, and weirdos). I am grateful as well to ace researchers M. J. Crowley and Jennifer Ewing of the *Inquirer*'s library for thoroughly mining their computer data bases for so many pertinent articles and news stories.

My agent, Philippa "Flip" Brophy, responded to the story with enthusiasm and quickly brought it to the attention of the right person — Henry Ferris, senior editor at Houghton Mifflin. Smarting from his own brushes with incompetence, Henry was keenly interested in the subject. During our first meeting, he shrewdly analyzed the strengths and weaknesses of my thesis and offered several useful ideas for expanding it into a book. Throughout the writing and editing process, he showed patience, humor, and sage instincts about what to say and how to say it. In the end, through gentle guidance and deft editing, he helped me turn a rather rough-hewn manuscript into something both he and I could be proud of.

In preparing this book, I benefited tremendously from the knowledge and wisdom of others, many of whom spent hours with me discussing the subject and sharing their insights. Especially helpful were Elijah Anderson, professor of sociology at the University of Pennsylvania; E. Digby Baltzell, retired professor of sociology at the University of Pennsylvania; David G. Blankenhorn, president of the Institute for American Values; Hollace Bluitt, adjunct professor of political science at Glassboro State College; David R. Boldt, editor of the *Inquirer*'s editorial page; Noel A. Cazenave, associate professor of sociology at Temple University; James L. Crawford, Jr., headmaster of the Episcopal Academy; Susan C. Day, physician at the Hospital of the University of Pennsylvania and vice president of the American Board of Internal Medicine; Dolores Dougherty; Robert Eisenberger, professor of psychology at the University of Delaware; Amitai Etzioni, professor of sociology at George Washington University; Jacob P. Hart, partner at Schnader, Harrison, Segal & Lewis; Larry Hirschhorn, consultant with the Wharton Center for Applied Research; the Very Reverend Stephen Kent Jacobson, rector of St. David's Episcopal Church; Christopher Lasch, professor of history at the University of Rochester; Joseph Pell Lombardi, architect, developer, and historical preservationist; David Popenoe, professor of sociology at Rutgers University; Samuel H. Preston, professor of sociology and a specialist in demography at the University of Pennsylvania; Uwe E. Reinhardt, professor of political economy at Princeton University; Jim and Tanya Walters; Mary Walton, staff writer for the *Inquirer Magazine* and an expert on W. Edwards Deming and the quality movement; and Ross A. Webber, professor of management at the Wharton School. After the manuscript was finished, I showed certain portions I was unsure about to a few trusted associates and friends. I deeply appreciate the savvy advice and sound suggestions of Roger Cohn, Gil Gaul, Marc Kaufman, and Bill Marimow.

Finally, I never could have completed this book without the love, assistance, and encouragement of two people: my wife, Tanya, and my grandfather, Edward A. Lynch. For nearly a year my wife has been married to a man who was either working or so preoccupied, exhausted, and moody that he was anything but a pleasure to live with. She bore it all with amazing grace, relieving me of many responsibilities and doing all she could to enable me to concentrate on this book with a minimum of distraction and interruption. (My son, Teddy, deserves plenty of credit too for good-naturedly tolerating a daddy who for several months was almost always too busy to play with him.)

As for my grandfather, he's been a guiding light, inspiration, and advocate for so long that I can't begin to thank him. Working on this book deprived both of us of many hours of pleasure together. But he never complained. Instead he was unstinting in his support. I hope that what I've produced makes the sacrifice seem worth it.

Bibliography

Adler, Jerry. "Taking Offense: Is This the New Enlightenment on Campus or the New McCarthyism?" *Newsweek*, December 24, 1990.

Begley, Sharon. "Heaven Can Wait: A Flawed Mirror Blurs the Vision of the $1.5 Billion Hubble Telescope, Imperiling Its Hopes of Seeing to the Edge of Space and the Beginning of Time." *Newsweek*, July 9, 1990.

Bennett, William J. *American Education: Making It Work*. Washington, D.C.: U.S. Department of Education, 1988.

Berger, Brigitte, and Berger, Peter L. *The War over the Family*. New York: Anchor Press/Doubleday, 1983.

Berger, Joseph. "Principals' Union and Fernandez in Accord to Shift Incompetents." *New York Times*, March 9, 1990.

Bjerklie, David. "Roots of the Hubble's Troubles." *Time*, December 10, 1990.

Blankenhorn, David. "How to Think about the Family: Ten Suggestions." *First Things, a Monthly Journal of Religion and Public Life*, August/September 1990.

Blonston, Gary. "Why the U.S. Keeps Dropping the Technological Ball." *Philadelphia Inquirer*, May 13, 1990.

Bloom, Allan. *The Closing of the American Mind*. New York: Touchstone Books/Simon & Schuster, 1988.

Boldt, David R. "Even America's Best and Brightest Aren't That Good." *Philadelphia Inquirer*, February 4, 1990.

———. "Why Are American Kids Dumber Than Japanese Kids?" *Philadelphia Inquirer*, September 30, 1990.

Bolte, Gisela. "Will Americans Work for $5 a Day?: An Interview with William Brock." *Time*, July 23, 1990.

Boyer, Ernest L., and Carnegie Foundation for the Advancement of

Teaching. *High School: A Report on Secondary Education in America.* New York: Harper Colophon, 1985.

Boyer, Ernest L., and Carnegie Foundation for the Advancement of Teaching. *College: The Undergraduate Experience in America.* New York: Perennial Library/Harper & Row, 1988.

Burgess, John. "Can U.S. Get Things Right Anymore?" *Washington Post,* July 3, 1990.

Carey, Art. *In Defense of Marriage.* New York: Walker, 1984

Carnegie Foundation for the Advancement of Teaching. *Campus Life: In Search of Community.* Princeton: Princeton University Press, 1990.

———. *An Imperiled Generation: Saving Urban Schools.* Princeton: Princeton University Press, 1988.

Cherlin, Andrew. "Recent Changes in American Fertility, Marriage, and Divorce." *Annals of the American Academy of Political and Social Science,* July 1990.

Cloud, Stanley W. "The Can't Do Government: Paralyzed by Special Interests and Shortsightedness, Washington No Longer Seems Capable of Responding to Its Growing Challenges." *Time,* October 23, 1989.

———. "Nothing to Cheer: The Biggest Casualty of the Midterm Election May Be George Bush." *Time,* November 19, 1990.

Cohen, Richard. "As Unfeeling as They Wanna Be." *Washington Post Magazine,* July 1, 1990.

College Entrance Examination Board. *On Further Examination: Report of the Advisory Panel on the Scholastic Aptitude Test Score Decline.* New York: College Entrance Examination Board, 1977.

Commission on the Skills of the American Workforce. *America's Choice: High Skills or Low Wages!* Rochester, N.Y.: National Center on Education and the Economy, 1990.

Cooper, Kenneth J. "Tests of U.S. Students Show Little Progress: Cavazos Criticizes Education Reforms of '80s." *Washington Post,* January 10, 1989.

Corliss, Richard. "X-Rated." *Time,* May 7, 1990.

Council on Competitiveness. *America's Competitive Crisis: Confronting the New Reality.* Washington, D.C.: Council on Competitiveness, 1987.

———. *Competitiveness Index 1990.* Washington, D.C.: Council on Competitiveness, 1990.

Cousins, Norman. "The Decline of Neatness." *Time,* April 2, 1990.

Critchfield, Richard. *An American Looks at Britain.* New York: Doubleday, 1990.

Darman, Richard G. "Beyond the Deficit Problem: 'Now-Nowism' and 'The New Balance.' " Address to the National Press Club, Washington, D.C., July 20, 1989.

Drake, Donald. "The Lost Generation: An Addict's Need for Crack Is Stronger Than Any Human Instinct — Stronger Even Than a Mother's Love." *Philadelphia Inquirer Magazine,* July 23, 1989.

Eisenberger, Robert. *Blue Monday: The Loss of the Work Ethic in America.* New York: Paragon House, 1989.

Ellis, Bret Easton. *American Psycho.* New York: Vintage Books, 1991.

Everett, David. "Taking Some Shine Off Cadillac's 1st-Place Finish." *Philadelphia Inquirer,* December 14, 1990.

Fairlie, Henry. "Fear of Living: America's Morbid Aversion to Risk." *New Republic,* January 23, 1989.

Feldstein, Martin, and Feldstein, Kathleen. "U.S. Workers Meet Japanese Standards." *Philadelphia Inquirer,* June 12, 1990.

Fingerhut, Lois A., and Kleinman, Joel C. "International and Interstate Comparisons of Homicide among Young Males." *Journal of the American Medical Association,* June 27, 1990.

Fiske, Edward B., Berger, Joseph, and Schmidt, William E. "Skills versus Jobs: The Classroom Mismatch." *New York Times,* September 25, 26, 27, 1989.

Friedman, Edwin H. "Empathy Defeats Therapy." *Family Therapy News,* September/October 1988.

Fussell, Paul. *Wartime: Understanding and Behavior in the Second World War.* New York: Oxford University Press, 1989.

Gates, Henry Louis, Jr. "Learning the Language of Rap: Understanding Is the Key, Not Censorship." *Philadelphia Daily News,* June 20, 1990.

Gibbs, Nancy. "Shameful Bequests to the Next Generation: America's Legacy to Its Young People Includes Bad Schools, Poor Health Care, Deadly Addictions, Crushing Debts — and Utter Indifference." *Time,* October 8, 1990.

Gergen, David. "People Are Everybody's Business: A Conversation With Peter Drucker." *U.S. News & World Report,* May 21, 1990.

Gross, David M., and Scott, Sophronia. "Proceeding with Caution: The Twentysomething Generation Is Balking at Work, Marriage and Baby-Boomer Values. Why Are Today's Young Adults So Skeptical?" *Time*, July 16, 1990.

Gwynne, S. C. "New Kid on the Dock: Loaded with Technical Innovations, Toyota's Lexus Sets the Luxury-Auto Trade on Its Rear Bumper, a Sobering Portent of the Japanese Industry's Prowess." *Time*, September 17, 1990.

————. "The Right Stuff: Does U.S. Industry Have It? With Teamwork and New Ideas, GM's Saturn Aims to Show That American Manufacturing Can Come Roaring Back." *Time*, October 29, 1990.

Hollman, Laurie. "Cheats Abound, but SEPTA Is Fighting Back." *Philadelphia Inquirer*, July 22, 1990.

Huber, Peter W. *Liability: The Legal Revolution and Its Consequences*. New York: Basic Books, 1988.

Iacocca, Lee A. "America's Competitiveness in the '90s." Address to the Commonwealth Club, San Francisco, November 8, 1990.

Ishihara, Shintaro. *The Japan That Can Say No*. New York: Simon & Schuster, 1991.

Iyer, Pico. "History? Education? Zap! Pow! Cut!" *Time*, May 14, 1990.

————. "The Masks of Minority Terrorism." *Time*, September 3, 1990.

James, Ronald. "Too Many Black Students Are Using Racism as an Excuse." *Philadelphia Inquirer*, January 12, 1990.

Johnston, William B., and Packer, Arnold H. *Workforce 2000: Work and Workers for the 21st Century*. Indianapolis: Hudson Institute, 1987.

Jones, Landon Y. *Great Expectations: America and the Baby Boom Generation*. New York: Ballantine, 1980.

Kennedy, Donald. *Stanford in Its Second Century*. Address at Stanford University, April 5, 1990.

Kimelman, Donald. "Do Some Blacks Reject Schooling as Acting White?" *Philadelphia Inquirer*, March 6, 1990.

————. "The Norplant Editorialist Emerges and Offers Up Some Fresh Heresies." *Philadelphia Inquirer*, January 29, 1991.

Krauthammer, Charles. "AIDS: Getting More Than Its Share?" *Time*, June 25, 1990.

————. "Yes, Good Art Can Elevate Society — and Degrading Art Has Its Equivalent Effect." *Philadelphia Inquirer*, October 30, 1990.

Kubey, Robert, and Csikszentmihaly, Mihaly. *Television and the*

Quality of Life: How Viewing Shapes Everyday Experience. Hillsdale, N.J.: Erlbaum Associates, 1990.

Lapointe, Archie E., Mead, Nancy A., and Phillips, Gary W. *A World of Differences: An International Assessment of Mathematics and Science.* Princeton: Center for the Assessment of Educational Progress of the Educational Testing Service, 1989.

Lasch, Christopher. *The Culture of Narcissism.* New York: Warner, 1979.

Leo, John. "Polluting Our Popular Culture." *U.S. News & World Report,* July 2, 1990.

Littwin, Susan. *The Postponed Generation: Why America's Grown-up Kids Are Growing Up Later.* New York: William Morrow, 1986.

McOscar, Gerald K. "Law Has Lost Its Luster." *Philadelphia Inquirer,* October 12, 1990.

Manchester, William. "America's Strange Celebration of Mediocrity." *Los Angeles Herald,* July 18, 1978.

Miringoff, Marc L. *The Index of Social Health 1989: Measuring the Social Well-Being of the Nation.* Tarrytown, N.Y.: Fordham Institute for Innovation in Social Policy, Fordham University Graduate Center, 1989.

Morrow, Lance. "In the Land of Barry and the Pilots." *Time,* November 12, 1990.

Morse, Edward Sylvester. *Japanese Homes and Their Surroundings.* Rutland, Vt.: Charles E. Tuttle, 1972.

Moyer, Larry. "Let's Give the Comprehensive High School a New Life." *Philadelphia Inquirer,* April 29, 1990.

Mullis, Ina V. S., Owen, Eugene H., and Phillips, Gary W. *America's Challenge: Accelerating Academic Achievement — a Summary of Findings from 20 Years of the National Assessment of Educational Progress.* Princeton: Educational Testing Service, 1990.

National Commission on Children. *Opening Doors for Children: An Interim Report.* Washington, D.C.: National Commission on Children, 1990.

National Commission on Excellence in Education. *A Nation at Risk: The Imperative for Educational Reform.* Washington, D.C.: U.S. Department of Education, 1983.

Neely, Richard. *The Product Liability Mess: How Business Can Be Rescued From State Court Politics.* New York: Free Press, 1988.

Oreskes, Michael. "Profiles of Today's Youth: They Couldn't Care Less." *New York Times*, June 28, 1990.

Papathanasis, Tas. "Junk Bonds Have Littered U.S. with Failed Businesses and Lost Jobs." *Philadelphia Inquirer*, June 22, 1990.

Popenoe, David. *Disturbing the Nest: Family Change and Decline in Modern Societies.* Hawthorne, N.Y.: Aldine de Gruyter, 1988.

———. "The Family Transformed." *Family Affairs*, Summer/Fall 1989.

Powell, Bill, and Martin, Bradley. "What Japan Thinks of Us." *Newsweek*, April 2, 1990.

Preston, Samuel H. "Children and the Elderly: Divergent Paths for America's Dependents." *Demography*, November 1984.

———. "Children and the Elderly in the U.S." *Scientific American*, December 1984.

———. "The Changing Nature of the Family: A Demographer's Perspective." Address at the University of Pennsylvania, April 14, 1989.

Raspberry, William. "A 1960s Radical Exhorts Blacks to Get Beyond the Victimization Mentality." *Philadelphia Inquirer*, May 12, 1990.

Reinhardt, Uwe E. "A Game of Private Profit at Public Risk." *Princeton Alumni Weekly*, February 21, 1990.

Reitman, Valerie. "Wanted: More Engineers." *Philadelphia Inquirer*, March 5, 1989.

Sanoff, Alvin P. " 'Universities Have Fallen Down on the Job' of Teaching Values: A Conversation with James Billington," *U.S. News & World Report*, October 1, 1984.

Shanker, Albert. "Asking the Right Questions." Address to the American Federation of Teachers, Washington, D.C., July 21, 1989.

———. "The End of the Traditional Model of Schooling — and a Proposal for Using Incentives to Restructure Our Public Schools." *Phi Delta Kappan*, January 1990.

Smith, Page. *Killing the Spirit: Higher Education in America.* New York: Viking, 1990.

Sowell, Thomas. *Preferential Policies: An International Perspective.* New York: William Morrow, 1990.

Spiegelman, James M., and Nelson, Robert. "Let's Not Forget the Economic War." *Philadelphia Inquirer*, September 6, 1990.

Steele, Shelby. *The Content of Our Character: A New Vision of Race in America.* New York: St. Martin's Press, 1990.

———. "A Negative Vote on Affirmative Action." *New York Times Magazine,* May 13, 1990.

Strohmeyer, John. *Crisis in Bethlehem: Big Steel's Struggle to Survive.* Bethesda, Md.: Adler & Adler, 1986.

Sykes, Charles J. *ProfScam: Professors and the Demise of Higher Education.* New York: St. Martin's Press, 1988.

Taylor, John. "Are You Politically Correct?" *New York,* January 21, 1991.

Thompson, Mark. "Probe Uncovers Serious Flaws in Apache Helicopter." *Philadelphia Inquirer,* March 29, 1990.

Tuchman, Barbara W. "The Decline of Quality." *New York Times Magazine,* November 2, 1980.

———. "A Nation in Decline?" *New York Times Magazine,* September 20, 1987.

Waller, Douglas, and Barry, John. "Inside the Invasion: Six Months after 'Operation Just Cause,' the Pentagon Is Finding Both Successes and Failures." *Newsweek,* June 25, 1990.

Wallerstein, Judith, and Blakeslee, Sandra. *Second Chances: Men, Women and Children a Decade after Divorce.* New York: Ticknor & Fields, 1989.

Walton, Mary. *Deming Management at Work.* New York: G. P. Putnam's Sons, 1990.

Whitehead, Barbara Dafoe. "The Family in an Unfriendly Culture." *Family Affairs,* Spring/Summer 1990.

Wilford, John Noble. "Hubble Astronomers Add Up Their Losses." *New York Times,* July 3, 1990.

Will, George F. "When the Gentleman from Iowa Offered a Tighter S&L Rule, House Voted 17–391." *Philadelphia Inquirer,* July 23, 1990.

Williams, Walter E. "What Blacks Can Do for Themselves." *Philadelphia Inquirer,* January 12, 1991.

Yankelovich, Daniel. *New Rules: Searching for Self-Fulfillment in a World Turned Upside Down.* New York: Bantam, 1982.

Yarbrough, Anise A. "Children Are the Ones Who Pay the Price of the Feminist Movement." *American Family Association Journal,* August 1990.

Zoglin, Richard. "Is TV Ruining Our Children?" *Time,* October 15, 1990.

ABOUT THE AUTHOR

Art Carey, forty-one, is a deputy editor of *Inquirer Magazine*, the Sunday magazine of the *Philadelphia Inquirer*. Born and reared in the suburbs of Philadelphia, he was educated at the Episcopal Academy, Princeton University, from which he was graduated with honor in English, and at Columbia University's Graduate School of Journalism. From 1975 to 1977, he was reporter and features writer for the *Bucks County Courier Times*. He joined the *Inquirer* in 1977 as a staff writer; in 1979 he became an editor at the magazine. He has won several state and national journalism awards for his newspaper and magazine stories. Married and the father of a son, he lives in Wynnewood, Pennsylvania.